MAKE YOUR BRAND MATTER

MAKE YOUR BRAND MATTER

EXPERIENCE-DRIVEN SOLUTIONS TO
CAPTURE CUSTOMERS AND **KEEP THEM LOYAL**

STEVEN G. SOECHTIG

WILEY

Library of Congress Cataloging-in-Publication Data

Names: Soechtig, Steven G., author.
Title: Make your brand matter : experience-driven solutions to capture customers and keep them loyal / Steven G. Soechtig.
Description: First edition. | Hoboken, New Jersey : John Wiley & Sons, Inc., [2022] | Includes bibliographical references and index.
Identifiers: LCCN 2022024922 (print) | LCCN 2022024923 (ebook) | ISBN 9781119860341 (hardback) | ISBN 9781119860389 (adobe pdf) | ISBN 9781119860372 (epub)
Subjects: LCSH: Brand name products. | Product management. | Consumer satisfaction. | Customer loyalty.
Classification: LCC HD69.B7 S64 2022 (print) | LCC HD69.B7 (ebook) | DDC 658.5—dc23/eng/20220609
LC record available at https://lccn.loc.gov/2022024922
LC ebook record available at https://lccn.loc.gov/2022024923

Cover Design: Wiley

SKY10034446_062222

*I dedicate this book
to my beautiful wife, Lori, and my two wonderful children,
Andrew and Julia.*

Contents

CONTENTS

CONTENTS

CONTENTS

Introduction

When selecting a historical figure to quote at the start of a book, very few people have selected Lefty Gomez for that honor. That's likely because most people have never heard of Lefty Gomez. To be honest, if it wasn't for Google, I would never have heard of him either. It turns out that Lefty Gomez was an all-star pitcher for the New York Yankees and Washington Senators, with a career that spanned 1930 to 1943.

Once I discovered Lefty and his story, I came to appreciate what an interesting individual he was, both on and off the field. Born and raised in California, he signed with the Yankees in 1930 (after a short stint with the San Francisco Seals), playing throughout the difficult years of the Great Depression.

It wasn't an easy path at first. In 1931, the Yankees were concerned about Lefty's pitching velocity and his overall size – Lefty was a slender 6 feet 2 inches tall and weighed 155 pounds – so the team physicians followed the standard medical strategy at the time and extracted most of his teeth – this was often the first step doctors would take to cure general ailments, a practice that was abandoned a few years later – while asking him to drink three quarts of milk a day.[1] If you've ever needed a reason to appreciate the advancements of modern medicine, consider Lefty and his relatively toothless life.

Interestingly, the strategy worked, and through these early years of his career, Lefty established himself as an elite player on the team. In fact, he was selected to pitch in the All-Star game each year from 1933 to 1939. As the new decade began, Lefty began struggling with injuries, and, just as the United States was preparing to join World War II, Lefty bounced between the Boston Braves and the Washington Senators, while working for the General Electric River Works in the offseason, which, equally interestingly, was the first plant to produce a jet engine.[2] It's not clear if Lefty actually put his hands on the first jet engines being produced, but it's distinctly possible.

Beyond baseball, Lefty became a popular speaker, sharing stories of his time on the field with legends including Babe Ruth, Joe DiMaggio, Goose Goslin, Lou Gehrig, and Dizzy Dean. Known for his comedic wit, he would regale audiences with stories from on and off the field, and Lefty was honored in 1983 as the last surviving player from the 1933 All-Star Game. There are plaques commemorating his career in Memorial Park at Yankee Stadium and at Lefty Gomez Field in Rodeo, CA.

In full disclosure, I'm not a passionate baseball fan. I never actively played the game and never found myself invested as a fan in the sport, at a professional, collegiate, or prep sport level. I freely admit that I'd struggle to name the starting lineup of my hometown Colorado Rockies, let alone identify the best historical players from the 1930s. That said, it seems that Lefty Gomez should be a name that I know, given his fascinating story and history of proven successes. He's held as a peer to many of the greats of the game, and is a proud member of the esteemed Baseball Hall of Fame.

So, unfortunately, I don't know him, but interestingly, it turns out, I do know of him. Most likely, you do too. I, like most people, know Lefty Gomez for the quote attributed to him. What is that quote? Lefty Gomez is known for coining the phrase "It's better to be lucky than good."

BETTER LUCKY THAN GOOD

Without a doubt, I've been lucky in several ways. I have been lucky enough to build a career over the past 30 years that has been focused exclusively on leveraging emerging technology to create experiences that improve customer perception, loyalty, and engagement. While the technology has evolved dramatically, the concept of technology leverage has not. It has maintained a set of consistent themes: simplify, personalize, and accelerate.

I've been lucky enough to work with brands that span a dozen industries and over 20 countries of origin. I've helped brands enter new markets, attract new demographics, shift their socioeconomic customer core, redefine their customer's perception of the brand, and, most importantly, meet their strategic business objectives through compelling, intuitive, and distinctive experiences.

I was lucky enough to come out of school in the early 1990s, right as experience technology innovation was starting to accelerate. I also came out of school in the midst of a recession, so I was equally lucky to secure a position with one of the most innovative experience organizations of the time, AT&T's solutions business. This group was laser focused on improving customer experiences for global companies, and I was thrust into the center of this improvement challenge at the earliest stage of my career.

I was lucky enough to operate in a time of unprecedented technological growth. After hundreds of years of steadily increasing rates of innovation, the 1990s were the decade when the pace of change moved from a steep linear curve to an exponential explosion. During these fledgling days of the Internet, the experience industry wasn't yet working in the browser but, instead, was focusing on integrative technologies within the call center, developing experiences that improved the drudgery of dealing with the phone agent. Few things generated a greater sense of dread than the ubiquitous 800 number with its long hold times, gratingly bland hold music, repetitive hold messages, and circuitous interactive voice response (IVR) menus.

Once a customer navigated through the automation maze, they would often land with a live agent who didn't know who they were, had no insight into what relationship they had with the brand, and had no context of why they were calling. It was truly the dark ages of experience, and this pain brought plenty of opportunity. As we break out in the early chapters of the book, this is the foundation of digital experience design that shaped the strategies we still employ today.

I was lucky enough to engage in a graduate program that focused on the strategy, design, and technology of digital engagement, before digital engagement truly existed. Back in those days, it was called distributed platforms. True innovators were recognizing the potential, but given that Marc Andreessen and his group of visionary innovators had just launched Netscape, digital engagement was still operating on the fringes.

In 1998, I was lucky to be recruited into Deloitte's Customer Engagement group. Within months I was asked to join a small team founding and building one of the industry's first digital experience agencies, Roundarch, a funded joint venture between Deloitte, BroadVision Software, and WPP Group. I was young, hungry, and given the opportunity to build and operate a team tasked with identifying and defining the next wave of experience capability. It was an incredible time, and this team successfully deployed some of the first true omnichannel experience solutions for clients. We tracked customers' journeys with a brand from the moment they first engaged, and we built common identifiers that would allow the company to track and understand customer activity across every channel, including the web, the call center, in-person, e-mail, and direct mail (yes, direct mail was still a thing in 1998). We used this data to create compelling, personalized visualizations and content across channels, evoking positive emotional responses from the customer while streamlining and simplifying every interaction. Ultimately, we started leveraging the data to create progressive interaction strategies that maximized the value and longevity of every customer relationship. These concepts became the foundation of the modern customer relationship management (CRM) and Acquisition to Loyalty strategies that brands employ today, as we'll explore throughout this book.

After exiting Roundarch, I was lucky enough to be part of a team that launched, ran, and ultimately exited a fascinating start-up, Orchestria, which focused on the next generation communication channels and how to manage communications through those channels. Working with the founding startup team was an exciting experience that absolutely increased individual agility, as every day brought a new challenge that often dictated the success or failure of the organization. If that sounds sensational to you, the odds are high that you've not launched a new company in your career. It's a high-stress, high-adrenaline environment, and it stimulates a level of creativity and rapid analysis that is truly unique.

I was lucky to be part of two startups that delivered next-generation digital experiences for brands and customers, facilitating structured communications across new channels (e-mail, text, and web) that was previously unavailable and, typically, uncontrolled. It also introduced significant risk — sharing information or the possibility of delivering messages that were inappropriate, in violation of regulatory directives, or in breach of security protocols — that required serious oversight and management. Further, facilitating a dialogue exclusively in a chat interface required careful algorithmic control of words and phrases, as there's no opportunity to react to crucial clues such as facial expression, inflection of voice, or body language. Given the criticality of the experience in maintaining the relationship between brand and customer, toeing this line was essential, and it took considerable investment in strategy, linguistics, and customer research. More importantly, the impact of experience on brand definition — including the realization that experiences were starting to define the brand as opposed to exclusively reflecting the brand — started to emerge. We'll expand on this quite a bit in the chapters of this book.

After launching one more start-up, I was lucky enough to be given an opportunity to rejoin Deloitte in 2013 to assist with the build-out of Deloitte Digital in both the United States and worldwide. The catalyst for Deloitte Digital's early growth was the proliferation of the smartphone, including both the iPhone and the Android platform. Starting with two experience design and delivery studios in Seattle, Washington, and Denver, Colorado, the studios were expanded throughout the United States and eventually throughout the world, with each studio focusing on building engaging, intuitive, and novel experiences that connected customers and brands. The smartphone opened up remarkable new opportunities to build omnichannel engagement strategies, as the phone became an interactive computer in the pocket, providing everything from dynamic transaction services to location-based proactive notifications. With each passing year, new functionality opened up that introduced new methods of engagement and connection, and forward-thinking brands took advantage of this to separate themselves from their competition. This evolution and the shift in strategy that this technological revolution drove are covered at length in the book.

Much more recently, I spent a few years with the illustrious McKinsey & Company as an expert partner and with Accenture as a managing director, focused on consumer marketing and engagement strategies. Out of respect for and adherence to McKinsey's confidentiality standards and requirements, I will not be sharing specifics of any of the work that I completed at McKinsey, but this tenure did offer me an opportunity to better appreciate how global brands have evolved their thinking, at the most strategic level, about the impact of experience on brand and the impact of brand on experience. At Accenture, I equally had an opportunity to work with brands focused on both B2B and B2C experience strategies, running continuous testing and learning motions to gauge reactions within various markets and adjust the engagement strategy based on the real-time responses that customers had to our messaging and positing statements.

In my current role as an Executive at WPP Group, I've had the opportunity to work with some of the most creative people in the industry, who are in turn working with the savviest brands in their respective industries when it comes to distinctive marketing strategy. These brands are at the forefront of brand and experience strategy, recognizing the unique challenges that the post-digital transformation era presents. The distinctive approaches that these brands have been exploring serve as the catalyst of this book.

I am lucky to have been given the exposure to the clients, the decision-making, and the successes and failures of various experience initiatives. I am lucky to have entered the workplace during the advent of the most transformative technological revolution in human history. I have been lucky to have surrounded myself, throughout my professional career, with some of the smartest and most creative minds in the marketing industry. Finally, I've been lucky to have been given the range of opportunities that I've been given. Truly, I've been more lucky than good, and I am thrilled at the opportunity to return that good fortune by sharing these insights in this book. If nothing else, I found an opportunity to introduce both of us to the brief history of one of baseball's greatest players, Lefty Gomez.

WHAT TO EXPECT FROM THIS BOOK

Before we get into the specifics, it's important to set a few foundational tenets for the book.

First, this book isn't a tutorial on the fundamentals of brand or experience strategy. There are dozens of excellent books that cover both topics in deep detail, so if that is of interest, then I recommend that you explore some of them. If you purchase them through your favorite retail supplier, not only will that give you the best option for gaining depth and insight into the topic, but it will reinforce much of what we do in fact cover in these pages about the importance of experience. Personally, I would recommend accessing a site that provides a guided and progressive search of various titles, helping you to find the best results based on your specific style and needs.

Second, the objective of this book is to present detailed breakdowns of the journeys and strategies of top-performing brands as they've navigated through the digital transformation era to now emerge in the post-digital-transformation era. The focus of each brand example is to provide a representative example of a brand that adopted one of the recommended strategies in this book to leverage your experience to define your brand. The shift from establishing the brand through messaging to establishing the brand through experience is inevitable, and these techniques are methods that you can employ to drive success in this new era.

Third, this book references a number of brands across a range of industries. I want to be transparent in admitting that I highly respect and value every brand that is referenced in the following chapters. I've interacted with them, I've worked directly with some of them, and, most likely, I'm loyal to the brand. It's through this bias that I selected to highlight what they do, how they do it, and why they're a successful example representing the recommended approach and action. That said, I do not provide any insights into brand strategies or experience approaches that are not already available in the public domain, and I've tried to meticulously document any specific references and statistics so that you have the opportunity to investigate the source in greater detail. This is important to highlight, as I have had the opportunity to consult with many brands and their executive teams over the past three decades, and a critical tenet of the industry is confidentiality. While it would certainly make for enlightened reading to know the inner workings of various company board rooms and the inner deliberations of experience teams, I've never breached client confidentiality in my career and I certainly won't do that for purposes of this text. That said, there are many general insights that are not uniquely confidential to a client, and I will be providing those throughout this book.

Finally, this is a fun topic, and I hope that this book will maintain a light and fun tone. As I mentioned before, I've been very lucky throughout my career to be given the opportunities that I've had, and I've been equally lucky to have fun along the way. Life is serious enough – if we can't find opportunities to smile and laugh from time to time, it's a long journey. Hopefully this book will offer a few opportunities to make you smile, and realize the joy that this topic can bring as brands work to gain, retain, and strengthen their relationship with their customers.

With that, let's dive in.

CHAPTER 1

A Far Too Brief History
of Brand Strategy

When reflecting on the history of branding, many marketers often reference iconic brand positioning that has stood the test of time. Most people can name the brand that told us to "Just Do It." Similarly, people of a certain age know which brand to use if a package "absolutely, positively needs to get there overnight," and that same generation recalls which animal answered the question, "How many licks does it take to get to the center of a Tootsie Pop?" We all know that if you have a Coke, it comes with a smile, and, more recently, that a 15-minute investment in time could save you 15% on your car insurance. So many of these brand statements remain with people for a lifetime, and they've positively influenced countless engagement and purchase decisions over the decades.

However, as all marketing professionals know, brand taglines do not represent brand strategies. Brand strategy is far more than just the use of advertising and taglines to promote a product. Enterpreneur.com provides solid insight into what branding is: "The marketing practice of creating a name, symbol or design that identifies and differentiates a product from other products."[1] Even better, this aligns with the teachings of every great marketing program in business school: "Your brand is your promise to your customer. It tells them what they can expect from your products and services, and it differentiates your offering from that of your competitors. Your brand is derived from who you are, who you want to be and who people perceive you to be."[2] That's as well articulated as any Harvard Business School seminar, and hopefully it saves you the $223,000 that their highly esteemed program currently costs.

THE EMERGENCE OF MODERN BRAND STRATEGY

It's fair to say that the twentieth century ushered in the era of modern brand strategy. Great brands that still persist today, including Coca-Cola, Ford, Colgate, and Chanel, all launched in the late 1800s and early 1900s. Others are slightly newer but still iconic, including Disney, Procter & Gamble, Nike, and most recently but still pre-digital, Apple. Each offered a distinct and unique value proposition within their emergent category, and they each evolved that positioning several times over their history. Perhaps more importantly, each recognized that the brand positioning was in fact a promise, and that the experience – whether that experience was the experience of working with the product or the experience was the service provided by the brand directly to the individual – needed to meet if not exceed the commitment expressed by the brand.

While each of these brands is often heralded as the first in its category, the reality is that each of these brands launched into a market in which alternatives were available. Henry Ford, for example, is often identified by the uninitiated as the founder of the automotive industry. However, when Ford started his company in 1903, he entered a market that Peugeot, Mercedes, Oldsmobile, Land Rover, Cadillac, Renault, and Fiat were all operating in. Peugeot gets credit for being the first car company in the market, after spending several years redefining their company strategy. Peugeot started as a coffee company in 1810; switching to bicycles in 1830; salt, pepper, and coffee grinders in 1842; and finally, automobiles in 1882. They brought the first car to market in 1889.

As an interesting aside, Peugeot's first product introduction was a steam tricycle that was too unreliable for mass production. Clearly that's a topic deserving its own book, and I fully expect that someone will eventually bring a steam tricycle into the Las Vegas Gold & Silver Pawn Shop, leading us to all see it on the History Channel's *Pawn Stars* show.

Core to the automobile, of course, is the engine, and credit belongs to Gottlieb Daimler and Karl Benz, two engineers in Germany who never actually met, for independently creating the first modern automobile engine design. That, of course, led to the launch of the Mercedes-Benz brand.

Further, Ransom E. Olds is credited with making the first high-volume gasoline-powered automobile, the Oldsmobile Model R Curved Dash, which had a transmission designed by the Dodge brothers. In the first year, Olds Motor Vehicle Company produced 635 cars, and the Oldsmobile, as it came to be known, was the top-selling car company between 1903 and 1904.

THE INTERSECTION OF BRAND AND EXPERIENCE

Given that all these brands, technologies, and products were in the market before Henry Ford and the Ford Motor Company brand came into existence in 1903, how did Ford create the brand, and establish himself as the founder, that defined the industry? He did it by creating a distinctive product that aligned with a clear market need, and he delivered it with an experience that separated Ford from the competition. Ford's earliest brand messaging created an emotional contract with the customer en masse, emphasizing that his cars were American made, gasoline powered, and available at an accessible price point. The initial print advertisement for the Model C, released in 1905, was declarative and confident. The primary positioning statement was, "Don't experiment. Just buy a Ford."

The more expensive Model B was advertised in print with the bold positioning, "[At the New York show] Experienced motorists were in praise of Henry Ford's advanced ideas and the universal query, 'What has Ford this year?'" The question was presented as validation that "the Automobile world looks to Henry Ford for the ultimate perfection of motor driven vehicles."[3] Ford positioned itself as being the undisputed innovation and quality leader, with unparalleled power and comfort combined together in a superior design. When fused with their price point (ranging from $800 to $2,000 in 1903, which calculates to a range of approximately $25,000 to $65,000 adjusted for 2022 inflation), they were truly an option for the average buyer. The Ford Motor Company created a distinctive brand position of exclusivity at an achievable price point, which allowed them to dominate the early market and allow the average person to feel like an aristocrat when behind the wheel of an early Ford.

Ford's early success was not exclusively driven by a clever and compelling brand position, however. In addition to developing a brand that connected with a large market of American car buyers, Henry Ford's entrepreneurialism and pioneering innovation in manufacturing offered the opportunity to establish one of the most unique early examples of the impact of brand and experience fusion. While his competitors at the time, including Olds and Cadillac, sold vehicles through a catalog or an exclusive retail outlet, Henry Ford sold his first models – the Model R, Model S, and others – through a network of dealers that offered the customer an opportunity to configure the vehicle top to bottom to meet their needs, wants, and price points. The customer could touch and feel the product to understand the options in detail, and the dealer's salesperson was trained to uncover both explicit and unstated customer requirements, increasing the level of satisfaction in the product itself but also increasing the probability of a repeat purchase at the time of renewal. Added to that were his remarkable efficiencies in manufacturing, which let him rapidly optimize the assembly line. These improvements reduced the time needed to manufacture a car from 12.5 hours down to 1.5 hours, which in turn allowed the customer to gain access to their cars quickly. Ford wasn't quite as customization-friendly as the modern automobile brand – he was famously quoted as saying, "Any customer can have a car painted any color that he wants so long as it is black"[4] – but he was able to bring all component manufacturing into the single factory building in Detroit, which ensured that customers were sitting behind their customized Model T almost immediately.

The impact of this fusion of brand definition and experience optimization is clear: The Ford Motor Company sold over 15 million Model Ts between 1913 and 1927. In fact, at one point, an absolute majority of Americans owned a Ford. That's a remarkable feat in a short period of time, particularly when compared against 1903's total output of less than 1,000 vehicles. Ford maintained this market-leading position for a number of decades, but it ultimately lost focus on the criticality of the brand–experience intersection, which is something we'll examine more closely in the following "The Criticality of Experience" section.

Setting Ford aside for a moment, let's review another example of branding and experience being leveraged together to create outsized growth in the early days of modern brand strategy, the forever iconic Pan Am airlines. At one point – in 1970 – they were the largest international airline in the world, carrying 11 million passengers to 86 countries.[5] Although they were liquidated in bankruptcy in 1991, Pan Am remains a recognizable brand 30 years later, evoking a distinctive response in individuals of every generation, including those who weren't even alive during Pan Am's peak of operations.

Pan Am, similar to Ford, is a story of experience innovation. Their origin story is one of experience selling, a concept we'll revisit in Chapter 5, Selling Experiences, Not Products. Prior to their founding as a commercial passenger airliner, they were flying a mail route between Key West, Florida, and Havana, Cuba, a relatively straightforward 105-mile route over the Straits of Florida. While this business provided a steady source of income, the entrepreneurial founder and aviation visionary Juan Trippe realized an opportunity to address a key customer need during the prohibition era. Trippe and Pan Am began advertising, in partnership with Bacardi, this same route between Key West and Havana as an opportunity for the everyday American to escape alcoholic prohibition and enjoy some rum in the sun in Cuba.[6] This simple example of an experience-led offering quickly led to an expansion of the Pan Am route network to other routes in the Caribbean and South America.

Cleverly, Pan Am realized early on that the appeal of tropical destinations was on the increase, so they purchased a fleet of flying boats, or clippers, that could land in the water near destinations that did not have proper runways for commercial aircraft. Using this approach they created an exclusive travel opportunity that served as the fuel for rapid expansion. The Pan Am product rapidly became distinctive and unique, which is equally a cornerstone of successful growth strategy.

However, to his credit, Trippe was one of the early entrepreneurs recognizing that product distinction can be directly tied to the experience. As a result, he funded technology investments from the earliest days, and Pan Am is credited with many of the innovations that we enjoy today in air travel, including the establishment of the air traffic control system, modern aviation procedures, and the introduction of pressurized planes. All of these advancements were driven by the need to create a better passenger experience that amplified the Pan Am brand proposition of luxurious travel.

As an interesting aside, given that they were flying the clippers in the early days, Pan Am designed the pilot uniforms after the Naval uniform, which is why commercial pilots in the United States today still wear predominately dark blue uniforms. It created a further perception of the elevated flying experience that defined Pan Am in those early days.

For decades, Pan Am repeatedly identified opportunities to improve the flying experience while defining it across two dimensions: the actual act of flying itself, and the experience that the customer received as a result of flying. This multidimensional approach represents one of the first such intersections that we today take for granted. More tangibly, Pan Am established what today as global residents we would simply consider the standard of air travel.

They recognized the opportunity to bring air travel to the masses and were the first to introduce an "economy" class, with a separate level of experience and a lower price point.

Most importantly, Pan Am recognized the power of luxury on perception, using the early mystique of air travel to create a brand and experience fusion that was truly unique. From the chic uniforms worn by the flight attendants (they looked like they stepped right off the Milan runway onto the Pan Am jetway) to the décor of the interiors of the plane to the gourmet quality food served in-air, the Pan Am experience established the statement that "air travel is as much about the journey as it is about the destination." Pan Am continued to invest in experience for the next three decades, being the first air carrier to invest in jets (allowing them to travel both farther and faster – improving the experience of traveling), establishing pressurized air travel, which allowed their planes to fly above bad weather, avoiding uncomfortable turbulence, and being the first carrier to invest in a fleet of 25 747s, flying the world's first jumbo jet across the Atlantic, Pacific, and entire globe. It's easy to imagine the sense of elevated experience that Pan Am was able to create when the passenger, dressed in their finest attire, stepped down the jet bridge, onto the plane, and to the staircase taking them to the upper level of the airplane. Truly a spectacular vision, and the magic of the Pan Am brand was later captured and replicated in the TV series *Pan Am*, which aired with a star-studded cast for 14 episodes in 2012.

There are dozens of other examples that we can draw from, including the Four Seasons with over 100 luxury locations worldwide, Louis Vuitton and their flagship retail store in Paris, and Wynn Resorts' highest-roller treatment in Las Vegas or Macau. Luxury brands understood early that luxury was defined through the experience. The brand commitment – the brand contract – was defined by the experience and as such, the experience was critical to the brand. However, during this era, the brand was still defined independently of the experience itself, and once the brand positioning was communicated to the individual consumer, then the experience's role was to reinforce and confirm the brand commitment. Given most consumer experiences were single channel – the physical experience only – the brand-to-experience relationship remained sequential.

That said, it's important to note that, despite this list, not all historical examples are luxury based. Howard Johnson's roadside motel and restaurant became iconic in its own right more for its convenient and consistent experience than for any element that can be considered luxurious. McDonald's became an on-the-road dining staple due to the convenient and quick service. Cracker Jack caramel corn, with its oft stale product served in a box with a surprise toy providing about 15 seconds of entertainment, brought people back to the ballpark, as referenced in the iconic seventh-inning-stretch song. These are all examples of experience defining the brand, with the experience being the product and the product packaging more than something external to the brand. This reinforces the argument that the linkage between brand and experience is not a new concept – only a continuously evolving one.

So what happened to Pan Am? Driven by their exceptional brand perception, Pan Am was the dominant international carrier in the late 1960s, flying over 11 million passengers to 86 countries worldwide. It was a near monopoly, but with the continued expansion of economy class, there wasn't significant pushback from the market, as seats were available at reasonable price points and the experience itself was so pleasant.

When Boeing introduced the 747 jumbo jet in 1966, Pan Am was quick to place a massive $500 million order, taking delivery and launching the first international flight from New York to London in 1970. With passengers popping champagne and cheering in their seats, the wide-body era had officially begun. Unfortunately, the timing proved to be poor, as the members of the Organization of the Petroleum Exporting Countries (OPEC) imposed an oil embargo against the United States in response to the United States supplying the Israeli military during the Arab-Israeli war.[7] This led to a severe economic recession, greatly reducing the demand for air travel, and increasing the cost of fuel significantly. This dual impact was catastrophic to Pan Am's operations and balance sheet, and by the mid-1970s, Pan Am was reporting annual losses while accumulating almost $1 billion in debt. It was an unfortunate set of circumstances that in no way reflected on Pan Am's brand, model, or strategy.

It's important to note that, despite their dominant position as an international carrier, Pan Am had no domestic routes. Prior to 1978, the government established route networks and while Pan Am had the lucrative oceanic routes, familiar names like United, American, and Delta Airlines, along with dozens of now-defunct brands, carried passengers between US cities. As a result, when the economic recession of the early 1970s took hold, Pan Am didn't have the ability to fall back on lower-cost, higher-volume domestic routes to support performance, and they started to covet this opportunity.

Adding to the problem, when the airline industry was deregulated by Jimmy Carter's administration in 1978, other carriers rapidly swooped in and began securing international routes from the interior of the United States, cannibalizing Pan Am's monopolistic position. Delta Airlines gained an Atlanta to London route, and the now defunct Braniff Airways landed Dallas to London. Pan Am's model was under threat, and they were anxious to secure domestic routes in short order.

This impatience led Pan Am to make a strategic error when they seized an opportunity to buy National Airlines, overpaying for the company in an attempt to outbid Texas International and Eastern Airlines. In their rush to gain the domestic routes, Pan Am neglected to realize that National's routes appealed more to the leisure traveler than the business traveler, and other joint ventures, such as US Air/ TWA and Texas International Airlines, which went on to purchase Continental Airlines, started to chip away at Pan Am's market share. The brand also suffered a catastrophic blow in 1988 when Pan Am Flight 103 from Frankfurt to Detroit was destroyed over Lockerbie, Scotland, by a bomb that had been planted on board. Over time, Pan Am was forced to sell assets and divest profitable businesses, leading to its demise and ultimately its liquidation in 1991. Coming back to our old friend Lefty Gomez, Pan Am was good but it certainly was not lucky.

THE CRITICALITY OF EXPERIENCE

Both Ford and Pan Am are wonderful examples of brand and experience converging to create dominance in the early modern age, but let's explore a third example, The Walt Disney Corporation, which continues to teach us lessons on the criticality of experience in the modern era. Perhaps more than any other brand, Walt Disney embraced the idea that experience is critical in building and maintaining the emotional connection with the customer.

Disney's origin story has humble beginnings. Walt Disney partnered with his friend Ub Iwerks to found the Laugh-O-gram Fils studio in Kansas City in 1922, producing a series of cartoons based on fables and fairy tales. Their first big hit, *Alice in Cartoonland*, was released in 1923, and it was somewhat unique in that it combined both live action and animation. The success of this film launch led Walt Disney to move his operation to Hollywood, with the help of his brother Roy, who became a lifelong business partner. The Kansas City team soon joined the Disneys in California, and the company produced Alice films for the next four years.

The rest, as they say, is history. Mickey Mouse emerged in 1928, and the third Mickey Mouse release, *Steamboat Willie,* in 1928, put Disney into the lead position in the animated movie market for many years. The 1930s saw the introduction of many famous characters, including Donald Duck, Pluto, and Goofy, and Disney started producing in three-color Technicolor as early as 1932. Classics including *Snow White and the Seven Dwarfs* (1937), *Pinocchio* (1940), *Fantasia* (1940), *Dumbo* (1941), and *Bambi* (1942) showed Disney's creativity and innovation, as he took the risk of introducing full-featured animation films, featuring multifaceted characters rendered in full-figure animation, at a time when no other studio was considering the format. Perhaps more notably, and courageously, Disney introduced an element of horror into children's animation media, with antagonists and unpleasant scenes sprinkled through the films. Fortunately, in all cases, the good guys prevailed in the end, and the audience walked away from the film feeling better about the world, which was important given that these films were produced during one of the most challenging periods in US history, the Great Depression and US introduction into World War II.[8] Like Ford and Pan Am, The Walt Disney Corporation's early brand success was derived from the product itself, but their true distinction and elevation occurred when they incorporated a world-class experience into the brand.

That experience, of course, was Disneyland, which opened in 1955 in Anaheim, California. It was quickly followed by the larger Walt Disney World Resort, opened in Orlando, Florida in 1971. These theme parks became a cornerstone of the brand and the primary growth driver of the business through these three decades.

From the launch of Disneyland in 1955 through Walt Disney's and brother Roy Disney's death in 1966 and 1971, respectively, there was a relentless focus on attentiveness and consistency in experience, which continues to define this brand that has withstood every societal evolution, and a remarkable amount of internal organizational conflict, over the past 65 years. During periods in the 1970s and 1980s when Disney produced few films, Disney World emerged as one of the leading tourist destinations and kept the company afloat. The reason for this growth and success is indisputably the power and value of the Disney experience.

From the very beginning, Disney recognized that going to a theme park is a special occasion, filled with emotion and anticipation for visitors of all ages and backgrounds. For adults and parents, there's a sense of nostalgia and the joy of childhood, and for the children there's a sense of magic and the belief that they have truly entered another world. To sustain these emotions, and leverage them to build connection and ultimately loyalty to the brand, the Disney experience needed to be consistent and it needed to be flawless, as even a small mistake could break the façade.

While in the early days the park itself was enough of an experience to create that connection, Walt and Roy Disney's successors continued to evolve their customer engagement strategy within the parks, demanding a relentless focus on the guest's perception and satisfaction. After their deaths, during the 1970s and early 1980s, many people are credited with reinforcing and expanding the Disney experience vision, including Van France, Dick Nunis, Marty Sklar, and a host of others. However, one notable source credits Bruce Loeffler for putting together a team to define and implement the now iconic I CARE principles, following a pivotal customer-experience strategy meeting that was held in 1983.[9]

The I CARE principles of Disney still apply to the dynamically interactive omnichannel experiences of today, which is why I'm highlighting them here. They were truly pioneering and founded on the idea of intimacy and emotional evocation. These five principles, put simply, are as follows:

1. (I)mpression, which recognizes that every interaction, every message, every visual, and every action will influence the customer's perception of the brand. No one moment is more important than any other, and no moment is anything less than absolutely critical. This is a principle that virtually every brand must learn to embrace across every channel and touchpoint.

2. (C)onnection, which focuses on creating a relationship that evokes positive emotions in the individual, whether that be a positive emotion (capturing anticipation and channeling it into a fun activity, for example) or a negative emotion (e.g., addressing frustration with an efficient and transparent resolution). Applying connection together with impression ensures that the emotional connection between the customer and brand continues to strengthen with each moment, which progresses the customer from ambivalent to loyal.

3. (A)ttitude, which reminds employees that their personal attitudes toward the customer, the situation, and the brand will influence the connection made through every impression. This important principle extends into modern omnichannel design, where tone and attitude come through every aspect of the design.

4. (R)esponse, which reminds the individual that the speed, quality, and communication of the response to every ask, whether it be founded on a positive or negative request, is everything. When the customer makes a request, it's critical to provide a response that aligns with the premise of the brand.

5. (E)xceptionals, which is a bit more esoteric in definition than the other four principles. In essence, *exceptionals* refers to the individual's ability to embrace the experience and be able to deliver the right experience at the right time in every circumstance.

While each point in I CARE is obvious once articulated, it was truly innovative once released, as brands hadn't clearly defined and emphasized a strategy so clearly customer-centric before. Disney continues to reap the rewards of this experience investment. In 2018, before the onset of the COVID worldwide pandemic and associated worldwide shutdown, Walt Disney World hosted a staggering 157 million visitors with an equally amazing 70% return rate of first time guests. The magic of Mickey continues to persist through the Disney experience.[10] Disney's simple methodology continues to serve as the foundation of modern experience design, which now crosses channels, platforms, and interaction methods.

There are many other examples that can be cited as we migrate through the 1970s and 1980s. Several organizations, primarily in the service industries, recognized that the experience was the defining characteristic of the brand, and these companies took unique and exceptional steps to build, foster, and enhance customer perceptions, shepherding their customers through the relationship cycle from awareness through consideration to commitment and, ultimately, to loyalty. Many embraced a variation of the Disney I CARE method, while others used "surprise, delight, and accommodate" as a foundation of the ideal interaction paradigm. As technology advancements continued to accelerate, several brands embraced these innovations to improve the experience, while others remained fixated on the human-to-human connection, understanding that technology at the time couldn't replace the instinctive and instantly receive responses that an employee can provide.

As brilliant and successful as these experience strategies were, no one was able to predict the dramatic impact that the advent of the Internet age would have on engagement and experience strategies. The world truly changed with the dawn of digital.

CHAPTER 2

The Dawn of Digital

As we all know, the world changed with the Internet. Starting with the new millennium, brands quickly discovered that they were losing the captive audience. Today's branding is rarely defined by the tag line. Capturing the attention of the consumer, and the business buyer, has become significantly harder, as each year seems to bring new channels, new content sources, and new buying behaviors that brands need to understand.

For the past 25 years, this expectation has led companies to focus on digital transformation. Digital transformation started as a legitimate exercise in process automation and experience optimization, but rapidly became a catch-all term for all technology efforts, be that customer-facing, employee-facing, or process-centric initiatives. Companies invested in data and analytics, in automation and connectivity, in web and mobile solutions, and in a range of other innovations. Not all investments were in technology, either; processes were redefined, products were re-imagined, and pricing models evolved. While most companies have battle scars as a result of this patchwork quilt of initiatives, and not nearly every initiative generated the return on investment anticipated at the start, these efforts have increased the performance and productivity of virtually every industry. New companies emerged, rethinking the strategy, structure, execution model, and very value proposition of the industry itself. Digital transformation became digital disruption.

The path to disruption wasn't always obvious. The most famous example of disruption in the short history of the digital era, Amazon, had humble beginnings as an online bookseller. Apple started as a PC manufacturer and operating system developer. Netflix initially took on the dominant Blockbuster by sending DVDs to the home with prepaid return envelopes.

Further, not every example of digital disruption ended in success. Alongside all the digital disruptors and transformation stories, there are an equal number of examples of models that failed to recognize the potential, and the urgency, of digital. MySpace had the position currently enjoyed by Facebook. Kodak owned the photography market. The Yellow Pages was once a force in local market advertising. There was an array of local, national, and global telecommunications companies that offered a range of services including direct dial tone, long-distance voice connectivity, and managed data circuits between locations. All these companies have shrunk or dissolved as a result of the digital era. In fact, since 2000, 52% of companies in the Fortune 500 have vanished,[1] and more are on a path to rapid irrelevance.

The speed of disruption hasn't slowed either. Models are appearing that hadn't been imagined a few years ago, and technology advancements continue to improve. Market expectations and consumer behaviors continue to evolve. As discussed at length in Chapter 10, Looking into the Future, we're only a few years away from a society that operates partially in the physical world and partially in the virtual world at the same time. Brands need to be prepared to respond. However, before we get there, let's start at the beginning, for, as with everything, there are critical lessons to be learned from the history.

THE BIRTH OF THE INTERNET

It's important to remember that the pace of digital change wasn't instantaneous. For most of its nascent years, the Internet was more of a novelty. While the origin year of the Internet is a topic of debate (arguments can be made for dates ranging from the late 1960s to the mid-1980s), the Internet known to the modern consumer definitely emerged with the 1993 release of the Mosaic browser, which is better known by its eventual name of Netscape, by Marc Andreessen and his classmates at the University of Illinois. With this release, the Netscape browser and a dial-up modem were all that was required for anyone to access the Internet. However, even with the blistering fast connection of the 2400, 9600, and, eventually, the hyperfast 56k bps modem in 1996, content was the primary limitation, and most people were accessing Internet Service Provider (ISP) portal pages provided by CompuServe, America Online (AOL), and Prodigy.

Baby Boomers and Generation Xers have a memory of the earliest days of the Internet. It didn't start with a boom but with a whisper. Given that access was dial-up based for the most part, and given that the early dial-up connections were extraordinarily slow, the content available to the average person was pretty much text-based and fairly limited by today's standards. It included news and novelty, with only a small amount of value-added functionality. As would be expected, self-described computer geeks were the initial adopters and comprised the primary group that flooded the phone lines in the early days. For those readers who don't recall or weren't alive during this nascent period of Internet connectivity, I'd recommend watching AMC's brilliant series *Halt and Catch Fire*, which accurately captures both the wonder and the limitation of Internet capability prior to the introduction of the modern browser.[2]

Between 1994 and 1998, consumers worldwide were slowly discovering e-mail and exploring the potential of real-time electronic communications. Chat rooms, separated by topic and geography, were popular among specific subgroups throughout the mid-1990s.

AOL's ubiquitous "You've got mail!" became the title of a Tom Hanks/Meg Ryan romcom in 1998, where the two main characters meet in a chatroom and then start corresponding, anonymously, through chat and eventually e-mail before meeting in person. This was still early days, and, according to Pew Research Data, only 41% of adults had been online in 1998.[3] While this was an improvement over 1996, when only 23% of adults had been online, there was still quite a bit of growth to come.

ONLINE ADVERTISING BEGINS

During these early days, brands were focusing on their traditional methods of mass market advertising, building now iconic brand campaigns that were amplified via television, radio, signage, and print, with slightly more personalized communications being driven through personalized direct mail and in-experience marketing, often in correlation with early version loyalty programs. The art and the science of marketing had improved with the evolution of technology, mainly due to the increase in ability to consume and analyze data, but the initial launch of the browser didn't instantaneously transform the industry.

As might be expected, the early adopters of online advertising were technology companies who were appealing to, well, technologists. The first banner ad was actually attributed to AT&T,[4] which bought an ad in the banner section of *Wired*'s online magazine *Hot-Wired*. It had an outsized return, with a 44% click-through rate, and this caught the attention of several entrepreneurs within the industry who recognized the early potential. Recognition of the potential for targeted, rotational advertising quickly became a topic in the halls of marketing departments.

At the same time, two clever Stanford students, Jerry Yang and David Filo, recognized a clear challenge with the early Internet, which was its inherent disorganization. Unless the user knew exactly what to type into the Netscape URL bar, it was impossible to find content. In response, they created a directory service cleverly named

"Jerry and David's Guide to the World Wide Web." While that name certainly rolled off the tongue, they were convinced to rename the service to the equally clever "Yet Another Hierarchical Officious Oracle." Given that most people without a Stanford technology degree wouldn't appreciate such a name, they shorted it to the ubiquitous acronym of Yahoo![5]

Rapidly recognizing the need to monetize the Yahoo! portal, they started selling advertising on their relatively high-traffic site. Banner ads became popular as a result of AT&T's early success, but display ads around the site were part of the design as well. Shortly thereafter, in 1996, Doubleclick and other companies started providing ad server analytics that focused on personalization and measurement, analytics that remain the foundation of modern digital marketing today. In fact, Doubleclick is attributed as influencing Netscape, and another early search engine, Infoseek, with the creation of the cost per thousand impressions, or CPM, pricing model for digital ad placement. That's a model that is still employed in certain situations today.

PERSONALIZATION OF THE ONLINE CUSTOMER EXPERIENCE

In the late 1990s, the potential of digital advertising continued to evolve rapidly, arguably evolving more quickly than the technology itself. This is a common theme surrounding Silicon Valley innovation, and has led to the boom-bust cycles of the digital era. Clever sales teams waxed poetic on the potential of this new platform to deliver customized and targeted advertisements to individuals based on their previous history with the brand, both online and across the organization. The idea of the 360-degree view of the customer gained rapid momentum, with organizations scrambling to build data lakes and full warehouses that captured every interaction the brand had with the customer. This noble idea became a foundation of digital transformation.

On paper, the idea of single-customer data sets is a simple one. Once an organization defines how to recognize a customer – what the unique identifier will be (phone number, e-mail address, some form of governmental ID, etc.) – then each interaction can be documented, each transaction can be catalogued, and, overall, behavioral analysis could be converted into an algorithmic understanding of the customer.

During this early era of the Internet, there were several avenues of interaction to focus on, many of which remain relevant today.

Unfortunately, getting there was not a simple, seamless journey. In-person interactions, including in-store, in-branch, in-office, or, for B2B models, interactions with the salesperson, were the most fruitful and powerful opportunities to engage, and remained the foundation of brand reinforcement, but these employees were inconsistent in their willingness to engage with automated tools and provide the valuable notes that could facilitate an integrated omnichannel experience. Other customer interaction channels, including the call center, field service, partner support, and, finally, this emerging technology of the Internet, rounded out the front office at the time, and enterprises spent significant capital to implement technologies to capture every note, interaction, issue, next step, and resolution. This was then combined together with back-office data, which included the products that the customer owned, the total and incremental spend, the status of any open service issues, and other data points that helped to define the customer. The ultimate outcome of this was a tailored experience for the customer that began to define the brand, and the beginning of this transition from brand-led experiences to experience-led brand definition. Companies that were able to provide a truly personalized experience – capturing what the customer was doing online moments before they called into the call center, for example – began to set themselves apart as customer-centric organizations. Early adopters of this, including Dell Technologies and Wells Fargo as examples, started to separate from their competition and create a perception of increased intimacy and empathy with their customers. During a time of rapid technological adoption by the consumer, this recognition of technological adoption by brands was very well received.

If you were an active consumer in the market at that time, you'll recall the emotional response when you first discovered that the call center agent, bank teller, field service technician, or retail associate knew who you were and the details of your relationship with the brand. Oftentimes, they would be able to accelerate the conversation significantly, skipping forward to the specific need and, if truly clever, leveraging the data to develop an anticipatory profile of you as a consumer, combining that profile with a distinctive proposition to tailor a narrative and experience expression that would strengthen your connection with the brand. It was truly a transformative time, but one fraught with peril, and, unfortunately, enterprise IT departments are now nursing the many battle wounds realized by failed implementations and overhyped expectations. Technology takes time to catch up with strategy, and during the late 1990s and early start of this millennium, technology was losing the race.

In parallel, during these early days, a revolutionary technology was being introduced, one that would truly change the trajectory of marketing and experience for the next 20 years: the browser cookie. The browser cookie, a simple text file exchanged between a company's website and a computer when the computer first accesses the site, was initially designed as a convenience and, ironically, as a mechanism to promote greater privacy. Its inventor, Lou Montulli, was a young engineer at Netscape in July of 1994 – he was 23 at the time – and he came up with the general concept of the cookie after meeting with another Netscape team who were wrestling with how to maintain an online shopping cart as a user crossed multiple pages. According to his blog post, Montulli's priority was to avoid cross-site tracking, as the early Netscape team recognized the importance of online privacy and anonymity on the web.[6] Unfortunately, engineers from DoubleClick and most certainly other ad-server companies found a loophole in the implementation that allowed them to do exactly that, building profiles of activity tied back to specific browsers. While this sparked the privacy wars of recent years, in the early days it was a catalyst for marketing personalization, allowing the ad servers to serve banner ads reflecting products that the individual had been searching for. There was an undercurrent of questioning – *how does this website know that I was looking at that pair of shoes?* – but given the newness of the Internet at the time, it wasn't a significant groundswell.

This early-stage personalization paved the way for many significant functionality advancements within the browser. Amazon, of course, pioneered the art of personalized recommendations, creating communities based on demographics and previous interaction history. Starting with books, which are often subject to referral and recommendation, the idea of "others who bought this product bought these other products" quickly became a standard component of online commerce. Persistence of the shopping cart was another early adoption feature that allowed the cart to be saved by the consumer, and a second was cross-channel persistence – the ability to start communicating with the customer in one channel (e.g., browser chat) and seamlessly transition the conversation to another channel, such as the call center or in-person service center, without losing the specifics of the conversation.

These early advancements are germane to the topic of evolving experience paradigms because, like all innovations, they rapidly shifted from novelties to expectations. Once a single brand rolled out the capability, the marketplace expected that every brand in the category would offer the same capability. The age of unreasonable expectations had officially begun.

While the Internet was the most visible and celebrated innovation of the new millennium, for justified reason, there were significant innovations across the technology spectrum that helped to create the environment we operate within today. Data collection, management, and analytics experienced a similar renaissance during this period, led by Tom Siebel and Siebel Software's customer relationship management (CRM) revolution.

Siebel pioneered the idea of the single view of the customer, as discussed earlier, providing an easy-to-use interface for the input and access to customer data. Siebel's solution initially focused on the B2B sales motion, facilitating automated information sharing of account information across the organization. This was, again, quite a revolutionary concept since, previously, business organizations had to re-establish positions, conversations, and statuses each time they would engage with an individual or channel. Further, management teams lacked visibility into account and opportunity status. The value of this sales force automation technology was quite clear, for both the enterprise and for the customer. It also helped to establish an experience paradigm that would never be unbroken; the idea that every part of the organization – regardless of role or channel – should be aware of every conversation, every interaction, and every situation surrounding the customer.

It wasn't long before Siebel, and other technologies, brought this forward for the B2C market, much to the joy of the consumer. Brands rapidly realized that they had a rich set of customer data that was being underutilized, and that it could be leveraged to better respond to customers requests in the moment. Consumers discovered that, when they called into the call center, the agent had instant access to their orders, order status, preferences, open service tickets, and other information, all of which was presented on the screen through a "pop" generated by the caller ID of the individual or information provided via touchtone digits. Suddenly, savvy concierges at high-end hotels immediately knew the guest's preference of restaurant, and the car rental agent knew the type of vehicle the customer preferred to secure. Customer service agents at banks had the customer's most recent transactions at their fingertips. Technology companies knew what printer the customer owned, and could order replacement ink in seconds. Experiences started to define brands, defining brand premises with experience that focused on convenience, efficiency, personalized service, and exceptional care.

THE E-MAIL EXPLOSION

Another watershed moment occurred in 1996, when Hotmail was launched and e-mail was introduced to the masses. Prior to Hotmail, e-mail required access to an Internet Service Provider, such as

CompuServe or AOL, which, while intriguing to those predisposed to technology adoption, wasn't in the mainstream. Reinforcing that point, prior to 1996, it was estimated that approximately 1 in 10 people in the United States had access to the Internet, and that access, typically, was into a portal such as that provided by AOL.

Given this limitation, before Hotmail, the embrace of e-mail was relatively slow. CompuServe started in 1989 with proprietary e-mail, Prodigy introduced e-mail in 1991, and AOL fast followed in 1993, but total subscriber bases hovered around one million or so per service, a fraction of the total worldwide population. Hotmail changed that dramatically by allowing people to sign up for personal e-mail addresses and send messages back and forth in real-time to one another, using handles and the novelty @-sign. People quickly signed up to gain access to this new capability. By the end of its first year, Hotmail had over 8.5 million subscribers, and similar services from Yahoo! launched in 1997.

As might be expected, e-mail marketing grew as rapidly as e-mail itself. Interestingly, the first e-mail marketing blast is cited as being sent in 1978,[7] when Gary Thuerk at Digital Equipment Corporation sent an e-mail blast to 400 recipients as a promotion for his company's computers. According to multiple sources, this resulted in $13 million in sales, an impressive return in actual dollars but a far greater return when that amount is adjusted for inflation into today's dollars! The spam filter was introduced around the same time as well. In December of 1996, as an ironic campaign message, technology company Xoom sent a marketing e-mail to 6 million Internet users to advertise their e-mail robot antispam filtering tool. According to their founder, Laurent Massa, the campaign was meant to be a joke. Massa explained, "You hate junk mail, and therefore we're sending you junk mail, telling you to get our free product so you can stop it."[8]

The history of e-mail marketing can fill an entire book, but to summarize, it exploded as a marketing channel over the next decade. It was estimated in 2008 that spam e-mail, defined as e-mail communications sent to the user proactively without their request, accounted for 92.6% of total e-mail traffic. That number has reduced steadily since, and it's now estimated to be just over 28.5% of total e-mail traffic, which is still a significant volume given that there's estimated to be over four billion active e-mail users as of 2020.[9]

CUSTOMER EXPECTATIONS AND TECHNOLOGICAL INNOVATION

The introduction of e-mail introduced a new method of communication previously reserved for the written letter. Consumers and brands could now communicate with each other using the well-established written form, but they could send these communications nearly instantaneously. Expectations rapidly increased to a point at which the sender expected responses returned in near-real time, forcing brands to temper the expectations of this media while exploring how this method of communication could influence the consumer's perception of the brand going forward. Back in those early days, no one could predict the ubiquity of electronic communication and the immediacy of multichannel communications that were to come.

Consumer expectations shifted even further, with the greater expectation that communications, transactions, and requests could be completed without any form of human-to-human interaction. Further, the communication window shifted to 24 hours a day, seven days a week. Communication also shifted from voice to written text, adding a complexity previously unforeseen by brand and marketing teams. Words, phrases, and sentiments translate very differently in written form without the benefit of voice inflection, body language, or facial expression. Consequently, the experience delivered by the brand, particularly for those brands focused on high-touch service, seemed disconnected from the communication experience. Brands worked to equip call centers with e-mail response tools and changed their name to contact centers, reflecting the multichannel aspect of communications, but it was difficult to manage the experience given the sudden volume of communications coming into the center.

From this point – the start of the new millennium – the pace of experience innovation started to accelerate dramatically. Phones became smarter and with the introduction of the keypad, first on the Palm Pilot and soon thereafter on the Blackberry, communication paradigms shifted once again, this time to short message service (SMS) and private messenger services, providing even more of a real-time communication method via the written word. Suddenly everyone could send e-mail or text messages while walking down the street, riding in the subway, traversing the country by car, or even, in certain situations, while flying at 35,000 feet. Written communications started to morph into conversations, replacing the phone call and furthering the now ubiquitous concept of multitasking. Along those lines, web chat in the browser became popular as an augment to the call center, and more brands attempted to shift traffic to this medium as it allowed their agents to interact with multiple customers at the same time. Unfortunately, the same communication challenges that plagued e-mail applied to these forms of media and were exacerbated by the real-time expectations. Customers were frustrated by delays in response, and the introduction of early-stage AI-based chatbots made the situation worse. Brands were losing their position as the experience eroded, and customers defected to brands that were able to meet their communications expectations of real-time, always-on, hyper-responsive, emotive and, somewhat ironically, more human.

As communication capabilities continued to evolve, so did our ability to find content on the Internet. As previously mentioned, Yahoo! started it all with their Guide to the World Wide Web, but that was soon replaced by increasingly sophisticated crawlers and search engines like Infoseek, Ask Jeeves, Yahoo! search, Microsoft (and then Bing!) search, and the behemoth of them all, Google Search. As search engine capabilities improved and crawlers worked tirelessly to interrogate, parse, and catalog every page on the ever-expanding World Wide Web, search converted from a novelty to an indispensable utility. More and more, the search for brands, and the related awareness-building efforts, shifted from mass-market communication and brand-to-consumer awareness to the reverse, in which the consumer and the business buyer were finding the brand proactively through search. The brand's site itself would shape search results, as would prioritized keyword bidding – a technique known as search engine marketing – but equally the search results would be littered with individual blog posts, third-party review sites, and competitive content designed to steer the perceptions of the searcher. This will be expanded further in this book, as this is the foundation of the transformational shift to experience-driven brand definition.

All this set the stage for yet another technology-driven innovation that has transformed our modern society: social media. Reflecting on the last two or three years, there are few two-word phrases that evoke a stronger response, but reflecting on the origin, these sites started with basic photo sharing platforms and community building platforms, like Facebook, Instagram, and MySpace. Social media networking entered the business arena with LinkedIn, and then quickly we were introduced to short-form multimedia communication platforms such as YouTube, Twitter, and TikTok. In a short span of time, social media platforms transformed how consumers and business customers research, communicate, and perceive everything from brands to news events to even their personal ethos. What started as novelty sharing of our Friday evening outings and Tuesday culinary delights has rapidly transformed into a primary communication and content source platform for many individuals. Ancillary social media platforms such as YouTube serve as a first step in the brand evaluation journey for many consumers and business buyers. The influence that anonymous and known people on social media platforms have on consumers and business buyers evaluating brands is extraordinary, and, recently, it has opened up an entirely new industry in social influence. Individuals with no background with, connection to, or inherent credibility about a brand were suddenly elevated to become spokespeople for brands, and their recommendations, some of which are paid solicitations but several of which are opinions based on personal experience and brand perception, can have a dramatic influence on today's brands. This is another topic that is covered in detail later in the book.

These are only a handful of examples during a time rich with advancements. There was a technological tsunami of innovations that took place during this period, and breaking all of them down could fill thousands of pages. I've skipped over hundreds if not thousands of game-changing innovations that emerged during this remarkable period in our history, each of which has shaped the perceptions and expectations of both the consumer and the business customer. Obvious examples of innovation include recommendation engines, biometric recognition technologies, voice-to-text-to-voice, augmented reality (who can forget Google's failed attempt with Google Glass), and virtual reality, which is suddenly coming into its own. The concept of the cloud – distributed storage and computing capacity hosted by a third-party and available on demand – opened up capacity to virtually anyone at any time. Devices themselves became "smart," and the term *Internet of Things* entered the worldwide vocabulary. Vehicles became more intelligent, and devices started communicating with each other without wires. The pace of technology innovation, as predicted by Intel's Gordon Moore and others, continued to accelerate at an exponential pace, taking advantage of improved processing speed and transmission technology to introduce new capabilities.

However, one of the most important technological revolutions of the last one hundred years was one of the most recent, and it was introduced by a familiar source. That revolutionary innovation, as you probably expected, was the Apple iPhone. That now famous moment in 2008 when Steve Jobs stood on the stage in Cupertino, California, and introduced the iPhone led to the greatest transformation in consumer expectations since the introduction of the Internet.

Apple's introduction of a touch-based supercomputer that fit in the hand, the briefcase, and the wrist truly transformed the expectations of customer experience and how customers discover, evaluate, commit to, and remain loyal to the brand. By opening up this simple-to-use and universally useful device to third-party developers and to the brands themselves, companies were given a blank canvas on which they could redefine the capabilities that they expose to their prospects and customers, and with that, they could define and reinforce their brand in new ways. Apple's vision was supported by exponential improvements in both cellular technology – the transition from second-generation to fifth-generation data transmission via cellular towers makes more advanced capabilities possible – and increased acceleration of other foundational technologies, including faster broadband speeds, improved Wi-Fi bandwidth utilization, dynamic GPS access, and more, all of which opened up new possibilities. Even the continued improvement of the camera introduced new methods of interaction and engagement. As a self-proclaimed Apple fanatic, I've personally owned every version of the iPhone since its initial introduction.

Apple, of course, doesn't deserve sole credit for the mobile revolution, and there are equally impressive devices introduced by competitive manufacturers including Samsung, LG, Motorola, Nokia, and many others. However, Apple is at the forefront when it comes to innovation, and while they don't lead in global market share – that honor, as of 2021, belongs to Samsung – they still set the standard in modern experience delivery. It has proven to be the critical catalyst in the transformation of both consumer and business buyer expectations, and this has led us to the current state of brand management that will be discussed in the remainder of this book.

EMERGING FROM THE DIGITAL TRANSFORMATION ERA

We're already seeing the next set of innovations, and if history is any guide, it's impossible to accurately predict what the next revolution will be. However, what is clear is that we've finally entered an era beyond Digital Transformation. Outside of, perhaps, a remote yurt-based hospitality venture on the northern tip of Greenland, every brand has adopted digital engagement capability at some point in their customer journey, at some point in their employee enablement, and at some stage of their back-office process automation. Most have adopted the fundamentals, and several have redefined their models to embrace the seismic shift in thinking over the past quarter century. These brands will be not only viable but successful as we look forward to the next 25 years.

More importantly, digital capabilities have become somewhat invisible. We can all recognize this in our daily lives. With the exception of truly forward-thinking and novel capabilities, we no longer notice digital capabilities; we expect them. If an experience isn't intuitive, seamless, and responsive, we have become conditioned to abandon the experience and look elsewhere. While this reflects negatively on the brand, it's more subtle than that in actual impact. The consumer no longer consciously views the brand negatively – they simply move on and develop instant affinity for another brand.

This phenomenon isn't unique and exclusive to consumer brands. Business buyers expect a full complement of digital capabilities to support their evaluation, transaction, and servicing needs, and partners of your brand expect seamless digital enablement across all touchpoints. Even your employees aren't immune, and if you don't provide digital enablement tools, data, and technology for every task, these employees will abandon their post and find a company that does.

Given this fundamental change in expectation and perception, we can now declare the end of the digital transformation era. If a company is still thinking about or talking about the need to begin their digital transformation, it's too late. The expectations are too high, the competition is too fierce, and the pace of change is too great. We've entered the post-digital transformation era, and brands, marketers, sellers, services, and employers must respond accordingly to capture and retain the attention and loyalty of the modern customer.

CHAPTER 3

Focusing on the Modern Consumer

$\mathbf{A}$s a proud Generation Xer born and raised in the 1970s and 1980s, whose first experience with technology involved an Atari 2600 hooked up to a 12-inch tube television, and who started programming in BASIC on a Commodore PET with an 8-bit processor, 4k of available RAM, and a cassette recorder for program storage, it's entertaining to take this walk down memory lane and reflect on the many shifts that we've seen in brand interaction and engagement paradigms. Even with those humble technological beginnings, I've remained current with all the changes and have fully embraced them. As Phil Dunphy proudly declares in the *Modern Family* Season One pilot, "I'm a cool dad. That's my thang. I'm hip. I surf the web, I text. LOL, Laugh Out Loud, OMG, Oh My God, WTF, Why The Face."[1]

The reality is that I, and many of my Generation X peers, pride ourselves on being technologically fluent and fully up-to-speed on modern interaction technology, but we have the luxury of memory of life before the web, before the smartphone, and before streaming content that tempers our expectations with brands. The Baby

Boomers and the Greatest Generation before them have even lower digital expectations, and in fact there are those who continue to hold onto the old ways of working and interacting. They still go into the bank branch. They still pay with cash, or, potentially, with a credit card, and they prefer to go to the mall to complete their Christmas shopping. They call the restaurant to make dinner reservations, and walk up to the airline counter to print their paper tickets. Not all of them, mind you, but many of the members of this generation prefer to operate as they have for decades. Smart brands recognize their value and continue to provide the quality of service, and quality of experience, that this generation expects.

MILLENNIAL EXPECTATIONS

The groups that matter, and the groups with the most potential to spend and to engage, do not share the perspective of Generation X. The most talked about generation in, well, generations, is Generation Y, more commonly known as the Millennials. The Millennials were born between 1981 and 1996, which, as of this writing, ranges them in age from 26 to 41. This is the prime buying age, and this is the group that brands are actively and continuously looking to attract and engage with, as they were estimated to have $170 million in purchasing power in 2021.

Millennials are often split into two cohorts: Old Millennials, who were born from 1981 to 1988, and Young Millennials, who were born from 1989 to 1996. This makes sense, as the expectations of these cohorts do vary widely given the pace of change that they've experienced. However, most notable is that, by the time Old Millennials reached adult age, the Internet was a ubiquitous concept. By the time the youngest of Young Millennials reached the same age of 21, they were in a world with touch-based smartphones, 4G cellular connectivity, and facial-recognition-based logins. These are truly the digital natives, and these generations have very different expectations of brands and experiences and widely different methods of engaging, decision-making, and committing than the previous generations.

As with many generations before them, there's a need to establish and maintain an identity that's independent of the previous generation. No one wants to be old and tired, and no one wants to engage with a brand perceived to be old and tired. While the young generation in the 1920s had flappers, in the 1950s had greasers, the 1960s had hippies, and the 1980s had punk rockers, the generation of the new millennium has digital natives. These digital natives are socially savvy, and they've developed communities online that have replaced neighborhood networks and other constructs. Savvy brands need to remain current in their communication and presentation to capture the attention of Millennials, while recognizing their other priorities.

Beyond digital connectivity, this is a generation whose view of the world has been defined by significant world events. This generation saw the direct impact of the 9/11 World Trade Center attacks and the continued rise of terrorism worldwide. They have lived during a time of bubble economics, with irrational speculations driving wild fluctuations in the stock market, housing market, and other investment areas. The Millennial Generation is the first that has prioritized experiences over asset acquisition, embracing the idea that quality of life is defined through experiences and relationships more than through the accumulation of wealth. That said, this is also the generation of financial risk takers who are willing to speculate in emerging concepts such as cryptocurrency and nonfungible tokens, or NFTs, two investment constructs based entirely on technology and not an underlying physical or operational asset.

Perhaps most fascinating are some of the statistics that Erik Qualman, author of *Socialnomics* and other books and currently an active keynote and motivational speaker, has cited over the years. Many of these citations reference other sources, but he's an excellent aggregator of these statistics. If you haven't read any of his books, I would highly recommend that you seek them out when you're finished with this one.

One statistic Erik Qualman often references is that 78% of consumers trust peer recommendations, while only 14% trust advertisements.[2] This isn't a reflection of advertising as a craft, but instead a realization that Millennials respond to how others perceive their experience with the brand, not how the brand articulates their experience strategy. Effectively, it's a "show me" mentality, forcing brands to overcome a natural skepticism that defines this generation. This has been driven by the proliferation of search and social media, which have led younger generations to access, rely on, and ultimately trust anonymous reviews as fact. Millennial consumers, and more recently, Millennial business buyers, will engage in dialogues on social networks that drive their decision-making and, over time, express their perception, and brands need to participate in this discussion, proactively, to control or at least guide the narrative. As Erik Qualman references in his 2013 *Socialnomics* video, when a minor earthquake traveled up the East Coast the year prior, New Yorkers received tweets about it 30 seconds before they felt it.[3] If news of an earthquake can travel faster than the tremor itself, it's staggering to imagine how quickly brand sentiment can shift within these social communities.

Millennials, as a generational construct, have several other consistent priorities, which include the desire to align with the cultural values of the brand – they want to know what the brand stands for and will engage with brands that reflect their personal values – and the desire to engage with personalized communications that respond to their situation in real time. They are interested in personalized products as well, and opportunities to customize an offering to their unique ask tends to separate a brand. This is the generation that engaged with the Coca-Cola Freestyle machine, which allowed young drinkers to mix any combination of flavors in their perfect soda drink. They're impatient, too, and expect that the brand will operate at their pace, skipping over any repetitive steps that should have been anticipated in advance given the individual's previous interactions with the brand. This is the data generation, having grown up in a world where brands have seemingly limitless information about their desires, needs, habits, and behaviors. In essence, they expect that companies will recognize who they are and anticipate what they want, but at the same time, they demand privacy and anonymity when it is comfortable for them, which is a fascinating dichotomy.

With each passing year, the Millennial Generation ages, of course, but this remains the most powerful group and will be so for the next 20 years. This group is at an age where they are getting married, having children, and settling into a true adult lifestyle. They are buying homes at a record pace, investing in markets, and progressing in careers, often into senior positions of considerable influence. As they mature, their behaviors may change slightly, but the fundamental habits of this group appear to be stable and will likely guide and shape brand experience strategies for years to come.

GENERATION Z EXPECTATIONS

The other generation of note is the emerging Generation Z, the group born between 1997 and 2012. This remains a relatively young cohort, but they are starting to emerge as a spending force in their own right, particularly on the older side of this spectrum. This generation is demonstrating interesting behaviors that will force brands to adjust their market behaviors even further, as their priorities diverge, at times, significantly from the generation of Millennials that came before them. This is the generation that was born with iPads in their hands, and as a result, they don't know a world without real-time access to content on demand. This generation saw YouTube emerge as the second largest search engine behind Google (both of which are owned by Alphabet) and they consume content through video and motion imagery. They're not inclined to read anything at length, and they fuse together the real and virtual worlds continuously in their lives.

Perhaps more interestingly, this generation, far more than any other, consumes content and experiences on demand. While every connected individual worldwide has become conditioned to accessing information – news, entertainment, answers to inquiries, etc. – in real-time on their phones, tablets, laptops, and smart televisions, Generation Z has taken this to a new level in terms of expectation. This group, without question, will be the catalyst for the end of recorded programming and printed content. They'll also be the accelerant for multi-channel, metaverse-enabled interactivity.

As Millennials age and start to settle into a more traditional lifestyle, Generation Z is picking up the mantle of experience pursuits, investing in multicultural and multichannel activities, ranging from travel and the outdoors to restaurants to physical activity. So while this generation is more digitally engaged than any before them, they aren't foregoing physical experiences – they are fusing them together in ways never before seen, which is opening up opportunities for brands to create awareness, engagement, and loyalty as this group's spending power, and market relevance, continued to increase.

THE CUSTOMER FUNNEL

All the generational cohorts are relevant to brands, regardless of positioning or market focus. It's critical that brands develop strategies for capturing the attention of each generation, inspiring the individual to engage and explore the offering and the value proposition. This is a continuous need, regardless of whether your brand sells directly to the consumer (B2C), to other businesses (B2B), or through other businesses to the consumer (B2B2C). It's crucial regardless of your distribution model, be it via a physical channel (such as retail or a restaurant), a direct digital experience (such as a captive commerce experience), or a marketplace (such as provided by Amazon, Alibaba, and a range of others). The opportunity to engage the modern consumer, including Generation X, the Millennial Generation, and Generation Z, requires focus and creativity at every stage of the customer funnel, recognizing that the modern consumer – both B2C and B2B – will expect unique and distinguishing experiences at every stage.

While there are variations in the labels applied to the customer funnel, most experts agree on the fundamental structure. For the purposes of the book, I'm using the popular structure of awareness, evaluation, transaction, engagement, and loyalty. In this structure, consumers start with awareness of the brand, where the fundamental value proposition is defined and the positioning statement is articulated. Quickly, consumers move to the evaluation and comparative stage of the funnel, investigating the specifics of the offering and validating the initial brand proposition. Once they've determined that the brand and offering align with their need, they then transact – committing to the specific offer. This can take many forms, of course, ranging from buying a product to signing up for an appointment with a healthcare service provider. Once committed, the consumer then engages with the brand and offering, further developing their perception and value proposition analysis post-transaction. Finally, assuming the brand is successful in the first four stages of the journey, the consumer converts to being loyal to the brand, committing to repeat engagement, providing a greater share of wallet by purchasing a larger array of products or services, and/or begins to actively advocate for the brand with others.

Again, this is a simplified funnel, and the intricacies of any company's individual customer journey will change depending on industry, offering, pricing structure, engagement structure, distribution model, and, of course, sales structure. The decision process to purchase a pack of gum while in line at the local grocer is very different from the decision process to procure a dozen laptops on behalf of a company. Both are different than the decision to set an appointment with a cardiologist to address a heart arrythmia, and each of those are different than the decision of where to eat dinner. However, in each of these cases, the consumer still starts with brand awareness, moves to an evaluation stage, eventually decides to transact, ultimately engages with the product or service that has been transacted, and then determines whether to be loyal to the brand.

AWARENESS

The first step in the customer journey is building brand awareness. This has historically been the domain of traditional advertising, with brands spending significant money to target large designated market areas (DMAs). This remains an effective method for building awareness and recognition, particularly for known brands and commoditized products. The reality is that, within a given market – Kansas City, Missouri; Birmingham, England; São Paolo, Brazil, and others across the world – there are significant populations of people with common needs. While the DMA is heterogeneous by design, the brand finds the common trigger that inspires the individual to explore the brand further (moving further into the customer journey). For example, automotive brands continue to leverage mass marketing to retain mindshare with populations during the time that the individual elects to purchase a car. It's difficult to predict, and therefore target, when an individual will be prepared to purchase a new car, so maintaining mindshare becomes critical. Not everyone will respond to every message, even in a relatively homogeneous market, but there are enough people focused on fuel economy, enough people focused on performance, enough people focused on quality, and enough people focused on distinctive features and capabilities, that each message has an intended result. It's a valuable strategy, and remains in place for automotive, consumer packaged goods (CPG), insurance, retail, and restaurant brands, where timing of decision-making is variable and brand awareness will significantly influence the next stage in the journey.

The limiting factor in mass marketing today is the fact that the masses are no longer collected in consistent message broadcast channels. Broadcast television, for example, is in rapid decline, particularly with the highly valued Millennial and Generation Z cohorts. While the older Generation X and Baby Boomer generations do continue to tune into their local news broadcasts and watch scheduled programming via local market and cable broadcast channels, younger people often don't even have access to these networks, instead exclusively subscribing to on-demand services tailored to their individual interests. They capture their news online, their sports via streaming services, and their entertainment on demand. Print and radio, while again still relevant in certain markets, are also in decline, and based on statistical and empirical surveys, the rate of decline is due to accelerate in the coming years. The days of mass market brand amplification are far from dead – it's still extremely important and relevant that brands reinforce their broad message across DMAs – but the strategies have evolved, the investment in niche market amplification has increased, and the consumer's response to the messages themselves has evolved as the generational mix has aged.

So what is the distinction between mass marketing and niche marketing? At the highest level, mass marketing broadcasts the general brand value proposition to the entire market within a geography or demography, anticipating that a certain percentage of the population will respond and react to the message. When Ford broadcasts an ad highlighting the new F-150 model, they emphasize a range of brand value propositions, from ruggedness to utility to fuel economy to next-generation feature functionality. This allows the message to target the broadest audience set possible, with the hope that it will generate an emotional response that in turn drives an action. With niche marketing, messages are broadcast to narrower, more homogenous communities, such as specific social media communities, specific streaming services, or specific content. As these platforms and services collect user data and viewing data, advertisers can define the specific subcohorts that they are looking to target. While more effective and efficient, it requires precision to maintain a return on investment (ROI) and attract a volume of customers to help grow the brand.

This opens up the value proposition of market analytics, a concept that is as old as brand marketing itself but which has evolved and improved in the last two decades as the amount of data available to the brand marketer has increased exponentially. Brands can rapidly survey different demographic, socioeconomic, and geographic groups to understand their wants, needs, and triggers. Brands can track purchase activity, both in store and online, and attribute that to broad demographic and geographic groups or, quite often, directly to the buyer. Between online profile attribution, loyalty program proliferation, B2B customer relationship management (CRM) and order-to-cash automation, and credit card data reconciliation, there's quite a bit of buying data available to the marketer to help identify their buying community and buying trends. Equally, data is available to track the effectiveness of higher stages in the buying journey, all the way through to the effectiveness of web and mobile display advertisements, social media insertions, and streaming advertisements, which can be correlated with IP addresses to the buying device, assuming that the broadcasting device and the buying device are on the same network. It's a rich time for marketers for certain. As this data is collected and evaluated, marketing teams can determine where to place their buys for maximum marketing return on investment (MROI), which can be further refined through real-time multivariate testing.

EVALUATION

Once the consumer moves from awareness to evaluation, the impact of 25 years of digital transformation becomes clear. It is at this stage that consumers have more control over the process with each new innovation in technology and content. As the brilliant Kaleeta McDade, Global Executive Creative Director at Ogilvy Experience, often says, "Advertising targets audiences. Experiences target customers." This has never been more true.

So what experiences have the greatest impact in the evaluation stage? First and foremost, there is search. Quite often worldwide consumers start the decision-making by opening a browser, either on their laptop, tablet, or smartphone, and interrogating Google, Amazon, YouTube, and other sources. The search may begin with a branded term (e.g., if I'm looking for a new winter coat, I might type in "North Face" or "Patagonia"), but more often it begins with what's known as a long-tail search, which is a highly variable, broad search phrase, such as "Best winter coats for Chicago weather in 2021." That may lead to a set of branded responses, including North Face and Patagonia, to appear on the first page of results, but it will also open up product reviews, influencer content, media articles, and a range of other results. Brands get in front of this by buying both short-tail (e.g., "winter coats") and long-tail terms, managing the search buy for maximum MROI. Given that, even today, 90% of searchers click on a link presented on the first page of search results, it's critical to optimize these bids. However, even with that statistic, search engine marketing in isolation is increasingly a diminishing return, as consumers look for new content paths before making the ultimate decision.

There are significant exceptions to the behavior just described, specifically in restrictive countries such as China and Russia. China has a unique and exclusive digital technology environment that operates behind the Chinese Great Firewall, and the Chinese consumer oftentimes starts their search on Baidu, an equivalent to Google with over 75% market share within the country (and a small amount of traffic from outside the country), and Chinese consumers access popular online marketplaces like Taobao, Tmall, and JD.com for product searches. Russian searchers do access Google, but unlike the vast majority of countries, Russian searchers equally use the local Yandex platform instead of Google. These are significant exceptions due to the population and economic strength of the individual countries, which matters greatly for global brands looking to penetrate the Chinese and Russian markets, but aren't relevant when looking at the rest of the world.

Historically, the science of search engine marketing (the bidding and buying of search terms online) has been somewhat straightforward. As of 2019, Google enjoyed over 92% market share,[4] so most investments in search engine terms were made on the Google infrastructure, and Google generously provided analytics that helped shaped the bidding decisions. However, over time, the amount of insight has reduced, and the search behavior has changed. While Google still dominates general search traffic, without any close second, more product searches actually begin on Amazon than on Google. A 2021 report published by Jungle Scout concluded that 74% of United States consumers start their product search on Amazon,[5] but an InRiver study maintains, in their November 2021 study, that the percentage of searches that start on marketplaces overall, including but not limited to Amazon and eBay, is only 44%.[6] More than likely, the difference is a function of geography – Amazon is still more dominant in the United States than anywhere else – and also due to methodologies designed to amplify different approaches, but the fact remains that more and more people start proactive evaluations via search.

The impact of search goes far beyond retail product purchasing, and it's important not to fall into the Amazon trap when considering digital strategies. The Amazon trap is the mentality that only consumer product brands need to focus on digital engagement as a critical component in the buying journey. Today, starting with search is the norm across virtually every industry, whether it be locating a medical specialist ("Hey Google, how do I find the best cardiologist in Dallas, Texas?"), determining which mortgage broker to use for my refinance ("What are today's jumbo mortgage rates?"), or which cars to explore ("What are the most reliable SUVs in 2021?"). Search can help to inspire ("What's the hottest restaurant in my area?"), it can confirm plans ("What time does the Avengers movie start?"), or it can lead to a comparison of products ("What's the best hiking shoe for muddy trails?"). Search possibilities are endless, as proven by the fact that, in 2021, 15% of searches in Google, which comprises over 500 million searches per day, had never been seen by Google before. The scale of traffic in today's market is staggering.

As you can see, the early steps of the evaluation stage focus on search, but they don't exclusively belong to the search engines and marketplaces. Other tools help with the evaluation stage, many of which are search-oriented in their own right. Examples of these include Healthgrades, which allows patients to search for doctors, evaluating both doctor credentials and patient reviews, and Yelp, which allows patrons to search for restaurants and, again, read customer reviews. Social media influencers provide product recommendations that lead to an evaluation, and in-home devices like the Amazon Echo will help guide consumers in specific directions. This early stage search evaluation is oftentimes an analytical exercise, so if your head isn't spinning from all the percentages and comparatives, a career in search engine optimization may be right for you.

Once the searcher is guided to an individual brand, the experience takes over. Tools that allow for rapid comparison, simple and transparent evaluation, inspirational guidance, novel guidance, and a compelling value proposition will keep the consumer engaged. Chapters 4 through 9 will provide ideas and examples for how to establish and distinguish the brand during this critical stage in the customer journey.

TRANSACTIONS

The next stage in the customer journey is the transaction. It is at this point that the customer decides to commit to the brand, which of course can manifest in a range of ways depending on the industry, business model, distribution construct, and other factors. Some transactional processes are quite simple – buying a snack at the convenience store or selecting the one-click purchase on Amazon – whereas some transactions are quite complex, such as purchasing a home or procuring high-cost items in a B2B construct. The critical trend here is the shift to online transactions and more specifically, to mobile transactions, with greater levels of automation, intelligence, and prediction penetrating every purchasing process.

For transactions, speed is a must. Digital experts prefer the fancier term of frictionless, but it really is about speed. In this post-digital transformation environment, there's no customer tolerance for complexity, there's no tolerance for errors, and there's no patience for multiform processes. Amazon pioneered this with the one-click transaction, and others rapidly followed suit. The information necessary to complete the purchase has to be minimized and should be captured so that repeat transactions are even simpler. That's the most significant evolution of commerce expectations, and it's table stakes.

Beyond simplicity and speed, there are opportunities to create distinction in the transaction process. Transparency, including real-time visibility, is one. Whether it be inventory levels, total anticipated costs, ancillary elements of the transaction, or wait times for services, the probability of generating a commitment increases significantly with trust, and trust is generated through transparency. Integration to modern payment methods is another, as younger generations have not adopted traditional financial instruments, such as Visa or American Express, at the same scale as previous generations. They are adopting digital wallets, digital transaction platforms, and alternative bartering solutions. Trials and phase-in models are actively reshaping product merchandising and pricing models, as consumers, both B2C and B2B, continue to be exposed to consumption-based models and try-before-you-buy commitment structures. As brands deepen their understanding of customer expectations and needs, the opportunity to drive distinctive differentiation and impact will become clearer, and it's critical that the transaction experience is updated based on that understanding.

ENGAGEMENT

Once the customer has committed to the transaction, whether that is a purchase, a sign-up, an appointment, or a reservation, the experience from that point forward solidifies their perception of the brand and its value proposition. It's stating the obvious, but it is important to reinforce over and over again that no written or verbal commitment from a brand will overcome the actual experience of interacting with the product or service itself and with the company that sold the product or service. The engagement stage of the funnel is what enforces the brand perception, and this stage will determine whether the customer is on a path to loyalty or a path to one-and-done defection.

This isn't a new concept, of course – it defined the iconic brands of the past including Ford, Pan Am airlines, Howard Johnson's, and Disney – but the rules have changed in the post-digital transformation era. Now the brand can't fully anticipate when, how, and why the customer is going to engage, and the customer will select a range of different channels within which to interact. If they have a servicing issue, or a product question, or a challenge with the current arrangement, they may reach out via social media, they may call, they may fill out a form on the web page, or they may download the mobile application. Regardless of the path that they follow to connect with your company, they'll expect that you have access to all of their history, relationship details, and relevant context around the inquiry. Further, the modern customer will expect immediate responsiveness regardless of channel, time of day, or geography, and they'll expect that they can complete most if not all tasks without the assistance of a live agent. The lines have blurred between realistic and unrealistic expectations, and the cost of not meeting these expectations is now greater than simple defection. The cost is defection and amplification, as the frustrated customer will now freely broadcast their frustration via the same public channels that drive the evaluation process, including social media channels, blog posts, and other media, which ultimately are picked up by the search engines. Continuous focus is a must.

LOYALTY

The good news is that it's not all bad news. As Newton's third law of motion states, "Every action has an equal and opposite reaction." While I'm confident that Newton wasn't thinking of the post-digital transformation era at the time that he defined his third law, it applies equally today. Yes, a poor response during the transaction or engagement phases of the customer journey will lead to defection with amplification, but, equally, a positive and proactive response will lead to unfettered loyalty and equal amplification. For all of the concern and negativity expressed about the younger buying generations – the Millennials and Generation Z – they have proven to be strongly loyal to brands that provide a positive experience at every touchpoint. That loyalty is strengthened with programs that expand their relationship potential, which we'll touch on further later in this book, but fundamentally they will continue to patronize brands that prove their commitment to the customer. Further, just as they will be instantaneous in their negative communications when responding to a poor experience, they are equally quick in expressing positive sentiments. Loyal customers can become your greatest influencers, expressing your brand proposition to their individual networks and helping your brand to go viral in a positive direction. Take advantage of this, encouraging this behavior, and you'll realize the results quickly.

Once a customer becomes loyal to your brand, the potential grows significantly. You'll have permission to build the relationship with them, encouraging greater engagement, greater expansion, and, ultimately, greater value between the brand and the customer. Clever marketing teams are continuously focusing on, and measuring, the progression of their customer base across each stage of the journey. Continuous testing and learning is key to success, which requires a restructuring of many traditional organizations to push empowerment and decision making down to the teams driving the day-to-day engagement. Equally important is measurement and analysis, with real-time dashboarding and dynamic listening tools tracking the sentiment in the market and the response that the brand is generating within key markets. These capabilities, which at one time were viewed as forward thinking and innovative, are now table stakes for brands. They won't differentiate your company alone, but they will provide the foundational capability that is necessary to drive the actions outlined in the remainder of this book. So, with that understanding in mind, let's dive into six opportunities presented in Chapters 4 through 9 for you to propel and differentiate your brand in this post-digital transformation economy.

CHAPTER 4

Believing in Your Brand and Redefining Your Strategy

In preparation for this book, I had an opportunity to speak with brand and experience experts in a range of roles and organizations. It's fascinating to learn from the stories they were able to share and the work they've done with clients. As I said in this book's introduction, nothing I share in this book reflects confidential information or insight gleaned exclusively from my team's work with them – every example provided here reflects this community's empirical assessment and publicly available data. Further, I've worked diligently to remain positive in all examples, as there's little value to dwell on negativity. While it's easy to highlight negative examples, and I'm a personal believer that we all learn from mistakes – I never fear failure – I don't feel it's necessary to highlight it in these pages. An intelligent observer can find the mistakes, and learn from them, on their own.

One of the experts that I had the opportunity to speak with at length in preparation for this book was David Mackay, a senior brand strategist at Ogilvy. David has a particular passion for this topic and offered tremendous insight into how forward-thinking brands need to define strategies for the post-digital transformation era.

One observation that David offered is that, today, brands are sometimes oblivious to the evolution, and impact, of experience and the importance of aligning the brand strategy to the experience up-front. He used the Matrix metaphor, from the popular movie, referencing the Blue Pill brands that believe they are fine with the status quo, and the Red Pill brands that recognize that they must make large moves quickly to remain relevant with the modern customer. Interestingly, in his view, brands rarely fall into the middle of the spectrum, making small and incremental changes, as those offer the least ROI. As reflected in Chapter 3, Focusing on the Modern Consumer, it's clear that the lines have blurred between realistic and unrealistic customer expectations and minor changes won't make a significant difference. No one will notice or react to the new button added to the mobile application or the new navigation on the website. Customers won't flock to the brand just because you added an Alexa skill recently, nor will they flood your brand with engagement because you allow for interactive engagement via their smart TV in real-time. Instead, the market will evaluate the brand across the entirety of the experience continuum, and unless every stage of the experience is aligned to the brand proposition, the one weak point in the experience chain will break the perception and lead to defection.

Most critical is that organizations need to believe strongly in their brand proposition and then evaluate and refine every stage of the experience to align in every respect to that branding. A perfect example of this, David highlighted, is Starbucks, which has emerged as an iconic brand that has stayed relevant through the many evolutions of the modern era.

EXPERIENCE DEFINES THE BRAND

Starbucks wasn't always the powerhouse coffeehouse brand that we know and recognize today. According to several accounts of their origin and growth, including an excellent outline provided by Britannica, Starbucks' original strategy was to remain small in operation.[1] They were founded in 1971 by three academics, Jerry Baldwin,

Gordon Bowker, and Zev Siegal, all of whom loved coffee and tea. For those of you who read *Moby-Dick* in high school or college, you'll recognize the name Starbuck as being the first mate of the *Pequod*. The three founders said that the name was inspired by the classic tale, evoking the seafaring tradition of the early coffee traders.[2] Even the ubiquitously recognized logo is that of a Siren, the mythical creature that was half bird and half woman who lured sailors to destruction by the sweetness of her song. To follow the origin of the Siren brings us back to Homer's epic poem, the *Odyssey*, but the original designer of the Starbucks logo, Terry Heckler, said he "sorted out old marine books and based the two-tailed Siren design off of a 16th century Norse woodcut."[3] So if nothing else, you can now correct people at cocktail parties when they try to convince you that the Starbucks logo is a Mermaid. It's not. It's a Siren.

In terms of the product, Starbucks was inspired by Albert Peet's Coffee and Tea, which opened in 1966 in Berkeley, California, and continues to operate today. Starbucks opened their first coffeehouse in 1971 in the Pike's Place section of Seattle – if you haven't been there, I'd recommend stopping by the next time you're in town – and focused on selling high-quality and unique coffee blends and brewing equipment. They weren't the café model that we know and love today. By 1981, fully 10 years after opening, they maintained four stores in the Seattle area, and had developed a cult following similar to what Peet's enjoyed in the Bay Area of California. Their head of marketing was a familiar name, Howard Schultz, but he left shortly thereafter once he recognized that the three original founders weren't interested in expanding their model to replicate the wildly successful café model that Schultz had observed during recent visits to Italy. They felt that the opportunity, and their brand, should focus on the coffee itself and not an experience that surrounds the coffee.

Thankfully for all of us coffee and tea lovers, the original founders decided to sell, and in March 1987 Schultz was able to buy the Starbucks brand and operation from the final two owners, Baldwin and Bowker. Schultz passionately committed to the café concept for Starbucks, with great results. He remained focused on the sale of beans and equipment, while adding other items to the store. In a short four-year span, the Starbucks chain grew from fewer than 20 stores to more than 100, expanding to Chicago, Vancouver, Washington DC, and New York. This growth continued after Starbucks completed a successful initial public offering (IPO) in 1992, and in 1996 they expanded internationally. By the end of the decade, 13 short years after Schultz took over, Starbucks had over 2500 locations in about a dozen countries.[4]

Without question, Schultz understood the value of experience and the opportunity for experience to define the brand. Starbucks' brand wasn't about the coffee or the tea, as the original founders intended, but instead it was about the warm feeling that you received the moment you stepped into the store. To repeat their own words, Starbucks "welcomes millions of customers each week and becomes a part of the fabric of tens of thousands of neighborhoods all around the world. In everything we do, we are always dedicated to Our Mission: to inspire and nurture the human spirit – one person, one cup, and one neighborhood at a time."[5] That's a firm commitment to a brand premise that is absolutely demonstrated through the experience that Starbucks provides.

When you enter a Starbucks store, both then and now, you are greeted by an environment that reminds you of the comfort of home, whatever that comfort may be. If the season is cool, a fire is typically crackling in the corner. If it's warm, there's a fan circulating comfortably cool air. Smooth, modern music is playing in the background, typically not loud enough to overcome the din of conversation. Comfortable seating abounds, and those seats are filled with friends and business colleagues enjoying a drink and a chat. Elsewhere, aspiring authors, including yours truly, are peering at a laptop screen and typing furiously. The décor is consistent throughout, with dark wood, glass counters, an array of snacks, and a consistent menu of drinks – the standard array of coffees and teas with perhaps a few unique options reflecting the local culture.

In this case, I truly speak from personal experience. Throughout my career, I've had an opportunity to travel extensively, visiting all

50 states of the United States and a range of countries including but not limited to England, France, Spain, Hungary, Japan, China, India, Russia, Australia, New Zealand, Brazil, Argentina, and Panama. In each and every case, there was a Starbucks logo somewhere near my hotel, and I found myself seeking out familiarity in the foreign land, despite the fact that I was in awe of the beauty and culture of everywhere that I visited. In some ways, the song from *Cheers* was true, that you simply "want to go where everybody knows your name." Not that anyone in the Moscow Starbucks knew my name, but it still had a sense of familiarity. The barista in the Mumbai Starbucks saw the jetlag in my eyes and gave me a five-shot Americano that I remember to this day. The Christchurch Starbucks had a guy on acoustic guitar singing Grateful Dead songs. The experience has stayed with me and my memories for well over a decade. The power was in the consistency.

It's positively brilliant what Schultz and his team were able to create. A consistent experience from store to store that caters to the local and the traveler alike, bringing with it a sense of belonging, of community, and of serenity. People integrated this experience into their daily lives, not hesitating to invest as much as $5 for a cup of coffee likely of equivalent quality to the local diner down the street, where the drinks are significantly less expensive. Many other large-scale coffee brands emerged during this time, including Peet's coffee, which inspired Starbucks, Caribou Coffee, Dazbog, and offerings within a larger menu of products at Dunkin' and McDonald's. Countless small, boutique coffee shops opened as well. All have accumulated their own followings and fans, and all offer quality products. However, the reality is that none of these have come close to approaching the following patronage or level of brand loyalty that Starbucks created through their end-to-end experience.

However, Starbucks hasn't been a single-trajectory-growth success story. Schultz retired from Starbucks in 2000, after their initial growth run, and for the next seven years, there was a period where Starbucks lost their way. As a case study published by Ivy Panda observes, the Starbucks experience became more impersonal. According to the study, by 2007, the idea of intimacy and familiarity had started to disappear, with fewer baristas greeting customers by name and large coffee machines hiding the coffee-making process. The case study goes on to explain that Schultz, who viewed human connection as the cornerstone of Starbucks' brand promise, had been lost during this time. Schultz noted that stores were no longer familiar in design, losing that neighborhood feel that created that emotional connection between the customer and the coffee shop. In simple words, Starbucks was commoditizing, becoming another mass-market coffee shop offering boutique drinks at a higher price than the corner diner."[6] Starbucks had briefly forgotten what made them unique – their brand proposition of the intimate experience – and their performance suffered greatly. The competitive offerings, including Peet's, Caribou Coffee, and the others mentioned earlier, started to develop parity of experience at a lower price point. At its low point in 2008's Great Recession, Starbucks stock dove to $6 a share, a 75% drop from their 2006 high.

Fortunately for Starbucks, Schultz agreed to return in 2007, embracing the idea of "believe in the brand and redefine your strategy" to deliver on the brand promise. In the case of Starbucks, this required that Starbucks again create a unique, distinct, and familiar café experience that would draw the customer in, but it wasn't about going back to the past. It was about embracing the future, and in his own words, "Creating the third place, after home and after work, where people will comfortably spend their time."[7] Schultz closed hundreds of stores, replaced several executives, negotiated Fair Trade deals, and focused on driving significant growth in China (opening the tea market for Starbucks significantly). He even noted that the food products that Starbucks sold created an odor that took away from the familiar aroma of Starbucks coffee, so he had the food items changed and the preparation process adjusted. Schultz recognized that people came to Starbucks to be productive and to be entertained, and more and more that involved electronic devices and Internet connectivity, so he was one of the first to offer charging stations and in-store free Wi-Fi.

Most importantly, Schultz and his executive team embraced the potential of digital technologies to again differentiate the brand experience.

BUILDING A CULTURE THROUGH DATA ANALYTICS AND ENGAGEMENT

What has made Starbucks a success story is their continuous focus on digital transformation and the opportunities that data and interactivity provide to improve the experience that every patron receives. This goes far beyond creating a convenient website and mobile application, which is the topic of Chapter 6, Time Is the New Currency — Anticipating without Being Invasive. It is the embodiment and fulfillment of the Starbucks brand statement, embedding itself in the neighborhood culture and inspiring people one cup of coffee at a time.

Doubling down on investment during a time of economic downturn required significant commitment and confidence, and Howard Schultz had this, both within himself and his new executive team but equally within the board and critical shareholders. After the 2008 recession, as part of the company's turnaround plan, then CIO Stephen Gillett created an "internal venture capital-style incubator for digital technology," called Starbucks Digital Ventures, and gave this internal team the autonomy to operate separately and build digital assets.[8] This led to the launch of the first Starbucks mobile app in 2009.

The mobile app was a critical launch for Starbucks as they were working to reestablish foot traffic in their stores. It leveraged an essential pillar of their brand experience strategy, convenience, to bring coffee ordering to a previously unimagined level. Launched in September 2009, this initial MyStarbucks app allowed users on the iPhone and iPod touch to locate a store through the app, access nutrition information for various drinks, and build their own concoction via the interactive drink builder. It even allowed for users to pay for drinks via the app in certain locations on the West Coast, which was a mainly unheard-of capability at the time. This new capability was both a novelty, which is an experience distinction strategy we explore in Chapter 7, Finding a Novel Approach to Solving a Market Need, and a foundation of the experience that Starbucks was looking to establish. Creating your drink, storing it in your application, and then using the app to push the order to the café so that it's ready upon arrival is as close as you can get to the experience of walking into your neighborhood pub and having your drink order waiting for you at your favorite stool. It was a genius move by Schultz, Gillett, and other members of the experience team.

The MyStarbucks app not only provided conveniences for the consumer, however. It also provided a wealth of data for Starbucks, as the application was tied into the Starbucks card loyalty program that was already in place. This loyalty program, which allowed users to refill a payment card and rapidly pay at the counter, was yet another element of convenience for the consumer that, in parallel, tied every transaction back to the individual. Starbucks began tracking the buying habits of the consumer and, by encouraging the individual to fill out a profile with basic information, could start to create customer profiles and personas that would ultimately guide decisions from store locations to menus to in-store operations. Baristas could again greet the customer by name, could offer suggestions and recommendations based on the evolving profile of the individual, and could make subtle comments that reinforce the personal connection between the server and the customer. Once again, Starbucks was beginning to feel like the home away from home, and it put them back on their growth path.

The MyStarbucks app continued to evolve over the next decade, with new conveniences and capabilities being added as the device capabilities, and network capacity, increased. By 2013, four years after its launch, the app was still driving 100,000 unique downloads per week, and Starbucks processed over 3 million mobile payments per week, generated by a community of 7 million active mobile payment users. This led to over \$3 billion in payments processed through the MyStarbucks loyalty card in 2012. The 10 seconds saved by ordering through the mobile app using the profile developed for the loyalty card cut 10 seconds off of ordering time in 2012, which translated to 900,000 fewer hours waiting in line across all users.[9] By the end of 2013, the stock had recovered all of its earlier losses and then some, topping \$73 a share.

LOCATION THROUGH DATA ANALYTICS

Building on the idea of analytic insights, Schultz and team recognized during this period of digital transformation that the individual consumer will only travel a finite distance for a cup of coffee, and any distance beyond that would degrade the overall experience, tarnishing the brand. Yes, there was a financial motivation behind this as well, since balancing maximum foot traffic with the cost of operating each store would optimize margins, but Schultz was relentless in his focus on experience, recognizing that experience would drive brand loyalty, which ultimately would drive revenue and margins. This initiative led Starbucks to create a Proximity to Buy model, leveraging data provided by Atlas to evaluate the characteristics of each neighborhood in which a Starbucks operates. The data set includes consumer demographics, population density, average income levels, traffic patterns, public transport hubs, and types of businesses in the location under consideration.

Starbucks continuously analyzes this data against actual store performance in similar locations to decide where to put new stores. It leads to decisions that may otherwise seem odd, such as placing four Starbucks cafés within one mile of Harvard Square or two cafés on opposing corners in New York City. Everywhere from São Paolo to Beijing to London uses these same models to optimize the store location, opening new stores and shuttering underperforming ones.[10] This model has become a foundation for store location optimization, but Starbucks remains a pioneer in using the data to optimize experience.

LEVERAGING TECHNOLOGY TO DRIVE ENGAGEMENT AND GROWTH

Starbucks continued to invest in their mobile and web experience. By 2016, mobile order and pay drove approximately 25% of total orders,[11] and this led them to implement their customer flywheel strategy in 2017. The customer flywheel is built on four pillars: personalization, ordering, payment, and rewards. Its goal at the time, according to Starbucks' Chief Strategy Officer Matt Ryan, was to "not only drive superior business results in the short term . . . but also make it very challenging for digital companies to outmaneuver us in the physical world." This was pure genius, and it continued to pay enormous dividends in terms of engagement and growth. By 2013, Starbucks had over 54 million active followers on Facebook, 3 million followers on Twitter, and close to 1 million followers on Instagram. As platforms later rebalanced, Starbucks redistributed and retained over 36 million followers on Facebook, 11 million followers on Twitter, and 12 million followers on Instagram. Schultz and team used this forum both to communicate with their customers but also to solicit ideas from them, and a solution named "My Starbucks Idea" generated 50,000 suggestions for experience improvements soon after its launch.[12]

Leveraging their internal digital incubators and suggestions solicited from their customers, Starbucks started building an ecosystem of partnerships with other innovative digital brands such as Spotify, creating unique playlists that enhance the Starbucks experience, and Lyft, making the process of getting to and from the café that much easier. They solidified agreements with the *New York Times,* the *Economist,* and the *Wall Street Journal* to allow content to be accessed via the free Starbucks Wi-Fi app, which encouraged customers to not just patronize the café but to spend more time there. As Adam Brotman, the Chief Digital Officer, was quoted as saying, "Everything we are doing in digital is about enhancing and strengthening connections with our customers in only the way that digital can and only the way that Starbucks can."[13]

That doesn't imply that Starbucks' investment in digital transformation didn't come without some speed bumps. The order-ahead functionality, in particular, proved to be problematic, as suddenly order volume increased substantially without the natural moderation that occurs when individual customers queue in line. Fulfilling mobile orders forced those in the store to wait longer to receive their drink, and worse, those in the store were watching attentively while the mobile orders were being made. Mildly frustrated in-store customers started to congregate near the order pickup area, and the overall Starbucks experience begin to again degrade. When some stores elected to prioritize the in-store customers, the order-ahead customers arrived to discover their drink wasn't yet ready for them, and they began to congregate and become frustrated. For a period of time, Starbucks became a victim of their own digital success.

Fortunately, automation and analytics again were leveraged to calibrate the Starbucks experience. Predictability models were created based on time of day, day of week, and the date, combined with real-time inputs such as the weather, to anticipate when surges of orders would come into the store. Baristas could then plan ahead, brewing and preparing specific drinks or drink components in anticipation of demand. Further, staffing decisions could be optimized to ensure that there was coverage for the order flow, without staff being forced into idle positions, and, in larger footprints, equipment could be moved into the back rooms, allowing mobile orders to be prepared behind the scenes in what have become known as ghost kitchens. These analytics also improved supply chain replenishment at the store level, ensuring that the individual café not only anticipated and prepared for the needs of the individual customer, but also had the inventory to keep up with demand.

Starbucks' 12-year digital transformation journey produced far more than just improvements to experience, a few of which were touched on lightly earlier. They improved employee productivity through automation of everything from scheduling to inventory management to product monitoring, and they increased throughput per store – total volume of orders processed over time – through automation. This, of course, led to a straight-line increase in both revenue and margin. They leveraged analytics, customer insights, and an agile testing philosophy to introduce new flavors (Pumpkin Spice Latte, anyone?), create seasonal and occasion-based offerings, and drive even greater engagement through digital marketing techniques. They've employed many of the other techniques outlined in this book and continue to follow this playbook to drive growth and retain their dominance in the market, even during the COVID shutdown period when their business model should have absolutely cratered. In all sincerity, this entire book could be based on the Starbucks story, as it is one of the best examples in the market of a traditional brand recognizing the importance of building a distinct experience, allowing the experience to define the brand. For purposes of this text, we will, for the most part, leave the Starbucks example here in this chapter, and highlight a few other brands that have followed an equally compelling path.

TURNING BRAND PROMISE INTO REALITY

Before we leave Starbucks, however, it's important that we reflect on what this means in today's post-digital transformation era. What can be learned from the Starbucks' story that will improve your brand experience and your connection for the customer? There are three critical lessons to highlight, all reinforcing the importance of focus and dedication to the brand.

First, continuously validate your brand proposition and validate that your experiences, across every stage of the customer journey, reflect that proposition. Regardless of how strong the brand and experience strategy, and how clearly and frequently the team articulates that strategy, there's always a risk that the focus on that strategy is lower at the point of customer contact.

Fortunately, it's straightforward to manage and measure the digital experiences' adherence, both through direct review of each interface, through customer listening tools, and through experience analytics. This needs to be a continuous process, and this review should be coupled together with a continuous improvement process. The Starbucks story reflects the impact of this, as they continuously identified opportunities to refine and improve the digital experience to support their overall brand promise and experience strategy.

For those brands that have a physical experience, be that a retail store, restaurant, branch, or other models, it's equally critical to frequently visit those locations. While there, executives and brand leaders should observe, visit, and talk to customers and employees, identifying opportunities for improvement and for alignment. Open-ended, high-level questions often surface remarkable insights and ideas while also engaging both customers and employees at a deeper level. Starbucks does this as part of their standard process, which led Howard Schulz to discover in 2007 that the reconfiguration of the store and the push to make it more efficient and standard was disconnecting the Starbucks store from the Starbucks brand promise. Further, the team's observation of how customers were using the store, and how employees saw the customers using the store. That led to tweaks in the in-store experience, and led to additions to the digital experience, to support that brand promise and keep Starbucks on their meteoric trajectory.

Second, don't assume that digital enablement will hide a poor experience. Focus on the brand-experience alignment described earlier and recognize that digital platforms and technologies are an enabler. As we've discussed, digital is now invisible. For the most part, it's no longer distinctive and it's like air; we don't realize it's there unless it's not. The Starbucks customer is easily frustrated if digital capabilities don't work as they expect – if their order isn't placed right, if their payment doesn't process, or if the Wi-Fi connection goes down – but these capabilities don't separate Starbucks from their competitors. It doesn't inspire lines that run 30 to 40 people deep at Denver International Airport. It's doesn't drive the full seating at the Starbucks in Christchurch, New Zealand, or on Kensington High Street in London.

Interestingly, if you comb their social media feeds, people don't rave about the taste of the coffee or the quality of the snacks, although both are, in my opinion, excellent. Instead, it's the perception of the in-store experience, the perception of consistency, the sense of home; this is what has continued to make the Starbucks brand distinct and unique, and Starbucks' relentless dedication to that experience-driven brand premise has allowed it to survive and thrive through two significant market events that would have destroyed many lesser brands.

Third, ensure your employees embrace your brand promise, as employees are the ultimate presentation of your experience. While I didn't highlight this at length in the earlier Starbucks story, it's been a cornerstone of the brand's success. Employees do not only smile and offer a friendly greeting when a customer enters the store, they try to recognize who they are and treat them as if they are a regular. This promotes the feeling that Starbucks is an integrated part of the community. Getting employees to the point where they wholly understand and reflect the brand takes focus and investment, beginning with an understanding of the brand experience strategy and then instilling the value of that strategy. Employees need to feel that they are part of something bigger, they need to feel that they are making a positive difference, and they need to be rewarded for exceptional performance. Starbucks does all three, and the result is a continuously positive in-store environment that connects employees with customers and with the brand, and drives deeper loyalty as a result.

CHAPTER 5

Selling Experiences, Not Products

Antonis Kocheilas, current Global CEO of Ogilvy's advertising business, has built his entire career on brand strategy, guiding many of the most iconic brands on their path of defining their value proposition and unique differentiation. Working with his teams and clients, he's won numerous awards, including the highly coveted Cannes Grand Prix award and several Cannes Lions for creativity. He also strongly believes that experience is foundational to brand strategy.

When Antonis and I sat down to discuss the focus of this book, he explained to me that brand strategy, historically, was an idealistic manifestation of differentiation. For years, agencies, marketing leaders, and brand managers would work to portray the individual brands as better than their competition, defining the unique characteristics, factors, and commitments that the brand offered above and beyond their competition. This is still the objective of branding today, and while the path may be evolving, the ultimate objective has not changed – the goal remains to create an emotional connection between the individual and the brand that ultimately drives loyalty in its various forms.

COMMODITIZED BRANDS BECOME INVISIBLE

In Antonis's view, the path of branding has evolved to the point that consumers and business buyers now engage with brands without focusing on what the brand is – the brand itself has become somewhat invisible. Antonis explains that we have moved from an age of "attention abundance and media scarcity," the age where there were only a few methods to communicate with customers and the customer was willing to pay close attention to messaging, to an age of "media abundance and attention scarcity." Thirty short years ago, the entire population of a city would consume their morning news from a combination of the local newspaper, the local news broadcast on the broadcast radio, and the local network broadcasts. These broadcasts were time boxed and controlled, and media buyers selected their audiences based on the demographic data of the channel. Now, there are countless sources of news and information available to every individual, without the border of time or geography, and it's impossible to predict where any given set of eyeballs will land at any moment in time.

Unfortunately, when you reflect on many marketing and brand campaigns throughout the digital transformation period and even today, it's clear that most brands haven't taken advantage of this trend. To the contrary, many of the brands have lost themselves. They've commoditized and fallen into a sea of sameness. Antonis compared this to the progression of automotive design in the modern era.

"Vehicle design truly transformed with the creation of the aerodynamic tunnel and the realization of the impact of airflow on car design and performance," Antonis explained to me. Once vehicle designers started to design for air flow and not for the unique beauty of the car itself, all cars started looking the same. It became difficult to recognize one car model over another – even the colors began to match. Similarly, digital transformation became the aerodynamic tunnel for brands, as every company worked feverishly to roll out online websites and mobile applications and create content shaped for the channels that appeared to be emerging each and every day. The result of this, Antonis highlighted, is that many brands started commoditizing their customer experience to match the customer's behavior. There were no distinguishing characteristics among them.

The result of this is that brand messaging, and the brands themselves, became invisible. The layout, navigation, presentation, and messaging all looked the same, and without the natural focus on individual brands that traditional advertising offered – it would be uncommon to see an advertisement for two competitive products back-to-back – suddenly distinction became replaced by blandness.

CUSTOMERS CONTROL BRANDING

The challenge of branding has accelerated due to the shift in control away from the brand to the individual. As Antonis told me in our discussions, "Branding is no longer controlled by the CMO [chief marketing officer]. Branding is now something that customer[s] do – the brand proposition is a result of the customer's engagement and not a result of the brand's communication." Whereas, before, the brand and the channel controlled the narrative and the style of communication, now the individual had the ability to bounce between sites, between channels, and between feeds with a click. In the pre-digital era, the biggest challenge that brand marketers faced was the remote control on the television or the push button on the radio, but now, suddenly, thousands of sources and feeds are available with the click of a mouse or the swipe of a finger. Brand advertising in the height of the digital transformation era went from an interesting novelty, when it was fascinating at first to discover that the advertising was tailored to my individual needs and wants, to a disturbing trend as consumers began to question whether their voice-activated assistant was secretly listening to their conversations and tailoring advertisements based on their casual conversations.

As a point of note, voice assistants don't do this actively; they're not monitoring your words and phrases to target advertising. They do listen for a trigger word – the most well known being "Alexa" and

"Hey Google," – and they will spot check random phrases to improve speech recognition, but outside of that, they're innocuously capturing the ambient sounds around them for no other purpose. As with so many things, the lack of accountability of modern media and blogging content has led to a set of runaway rumors that have unfairly diminished the value proposition of the conversational interface device.[1]

Regardless, privacy rapidly eclipsed the novelty of advertisements, and quickly these messages shifted from convenient to creepy. People started to react negatively to them, and as a result clever marketers tempered their messaging a bit to appear less targeted, trading hyper-relevance for comfort. In parallel, the primary advertising platforms – Google, Facebook, and others – came under fire for their data collection and targeting practices, again somewhat unfairly but nonetheless quite aggressively. Marketers more and more found their tools becoming tarnished, and suddenly the new and novel digital platforms became an unpredictable platform for brand advertisers.

REPLACING PRODUCTS WITH EXPERIENCES

So what does all this mean now that we've entered the post-digital transformation age? Do our strategies adjust again? This answer is yes, and that's the focus of this chapter.

Given brands have, for the most part, commoditized, during the digital-transformation era, the natural result is that products have commoditized along with the brands. One of the many impacts of Amazon's model is that everything now arrives on our doorsteps in a brown box, and everything is immediately accessible. Products have lost all tangibility. They've even lost their dimensions and sensations, being continuously displayed on flat screens and devices. It's hard to express the value of a lemon-fresh scent, or the unique softness of the cashmere weave, when looking at the product on a handheld tablet. Brands try to express the sense of motion and the sense of excitement through visualization, text, and video, but it's not the same. We're multisensory beings, and we're being reduced to one or at most two senses when interacting and evaluating products via digital screens. Now that digital has become invisible, we no longer view products with the same context that we did before.

Perhaps more interestingly, the emerging generations of Millennials and Generation Z are not emotionally triggered by the products, or even the brands, themselves. With perhaps a few exceptions – such as specific status clothing brands and high-end vehicle brands, which continuously and consistently capture the attention of young generations looking to reflect status and prestige by demonstrating their ability to acquire and own these exclusive items – this is not what creates the emotional bond. Younger generations are drawn to the experience of interacting with the brand, and the emotional response that the brand's experience evokes within them.

To put a finer point on this, let's focus on two well-known and admired global athletic brands: Nike and Adidas. Hailing from opposite sides of the globe, both brands have followed similar strategies, transitioning from product focus to experience focus to remain relevant and dominant through the digital transformation era and into today's post-digital transformation time.

A FOUNDATION OF INNOVATION AND PERFORMANCE

Adidas and Nike are interesting comparatives in terms of their history. Adidas is a 100-year-old company founded in Germany in 1924 by Adolf Dassler, with the support of his brother Rudolf, originally under the name Gebrüder Dassler Schuhfabrik, or "Dassler Brothers Shoe Factory."[2] Nike was founded 40 years later in 1964 by Bill Bowerman, a track-and-field coach at Oregon, along with his former student Phil Knight. Its original name was Blue Ribbon Sports. Neither Gerbrüder Dassler Schuhfabrik nor Blue Ribbon Sports were names that naturally captured the hearts and minds of the market, but then again they were named by shoe designers, not marketers.

Both Adidas and Nike started as companies with humble beginnings focused on improving the track and field shoe. Adidas, of course, was first. The Dassler brothers made their shoe in a small factory in Germany which struggled to retain electrical power, and quite often they ran their machines from power generated by a stationary bicycle within the factory. Dassler's unique value proposition was one of craftmanship; Adolf Dassler transitioned the typical track shoe from a previous model of heavy metal spikes to one utilizing canvas and rubber. Adolf and Adidas developed early fame after persuading U.S. sprinter Jesse Owens to switch to the Adidas spikes in the 1936 Summer Olympics, leading to four gold medals in the games. After that, the word spread quickly, and the Dasslers were selling 200,000 pairs of shoes every year before the start of World War II.[3] Notwithstanding a brief pause in manufacturing during the war, the Dassler Brothers continued to run their factory for the most part and are cited as being the last sport shoe factory able to operate in the country during the war. Conveniently, they were the predominant supplier of shoes for German army during this time.

Interestingly, and certainly not as well known, the Dassler brothers split in 1947, with Rudolf forming a new firm eventually branded Puma. Adolf stayed with the factory and the product and registered the name Adidas AG in 1949. There's an urban myth that the name is an acronym for "All Day I Dream About Sports," but in reality it's a shortening of the name Adi Dassler to become AdiDas, or Adidas. Three years later, immediately following the 1952 summer Olympics, Adidas acquired the three-stripe logo from athletic footwear brand Karhu Sports for two bottles of whiskey and the equivalent in today's money of 1600 euros. From that point, the brand-building started in earnest.

Nike followed a similar path, although it began not as a manufacturer but instead as a distributor, originally selling Japanese-made Onitsuka Tiger shoes, which Bowerman and Knight sold at track meets, keeping their inventory in the trunk of Knight's automobile.[4] In 1964, Blue Ribbon Sports grossed $8,000 in resale revenue, and that expanded to $20,000 in 1965. By 1966 they had a retail store in Santa Monica, and in 1967 they had expanded retail and distribution to Massachusetts. Knight moved to Portland and took over the business operations, allowing Bowerman to stay in Eugene to focus on shoe design. A famous story tells of Bowerman ruining his wife's Belgian waffle iron while experimenting with a sole design, which became known as the waffle trainer. The waffle trainer sole became the distinctive characteristic of Nike's first shoe, the Cortez, which was released in 1972. Even today it remains one of the Nike's most iconic footwear designs.[5] That same year, Blue Ribbon Sports changed its name to Nike, referencing the Greek goddess of victory, and the now iconic swoosh was first introduced to the brand in 1974.

In the early days of their history, both Adidas and Nike built their brands on the concept of innovation and performance, tying themselves to great athletic performances and the contribution that the shoe had to the athlete's achievement. In the 1950s, Adidas introduced the first soccer cleat with a nylon sole, their iconic Samba shoe design, which remained a foundation for decades. Their brand proposition was speed through design, and they tied themselves to the achievement of early athletic pioneers including Katherine Switzer, the first woman to officially run the Boston Marathon, and Dick Fosbery, who introduced the Fosbery Flop high jump style in the 1968 Mexico City Olympics. The implied statement is that if you, as the average Joe, buys an Adidas shoe, you can perform at their level of athletic ability. It was a brilliant and highly successful brand positioning platform. Shortly thereafter, Adidas introduced their first track suit, the Franz Benkenbauer, named after one of the most famous German footballers in their country's history – expanding their portfolio of athletic clothing products while continuing to tie their products, and their image, to iconic European sports figures of the time. Put on the track suit, don a pair of cleats, and you could be traversing the pitch just like Benkenbauer does!

Adidas expanded further, designing and manufacturing the FILA world cup ball in 1970, which they've continued doing ever since, and introducing their now well-known Trefoil logo at the 1972 Munich Olympics. Adidas shoes were worn by famed Olympians at the games, including the entire German team and, perhaps more importantly, Valeri Borzov of Russia, who became the fastest man in the world while running in Adidas shoes.[6]

The 1970s popularized an innovative tennis shoe – all white without the traditional three stripes – which, while originally named the Hallett (and introduced as such in 1963) – became the better known Stan Smith shoe in 1978. Associating the shoe with the American tennis star opened up the United States market for Adidas, as aspiring tennis players wanted to be associated with an American name. Suddenly tennis players and fashionistas alike were wearing the white shoe in the late 1970s. Finally, in the mid-1980s, United States hip-hop phenomenon Run DMC started to wear Adidas Superstars as part of their signature look, and followers of the band and hip hop fashion flooded stores for a similar pair.[7]

Nike took a similar path of branding, focusing, as one would expect, on American athletes. After introducing the swoosh symbol, which was designed by a student at Portland State, Nike released their patented Air technology, which was boosted by a rookie NBA basketball player named Michael Jordan. Just as the player did, the Nike Air Jordans took off, and every young person with dreams of basketball greatness rushed to the store to get a pair. I was one of those young people at the time, and I proudly donned a pair of red and black swoosh-prominent Air Jordan high-top basketball shoes in my high school gym, but, surprisingly, my NBA career didn't develop quite as I hoped. Fortunately, I discovered digital marketing and technology as a fallback option.

Nike continued associating their brand with great athletes, following the Adidas branding playbook of associating their products with elite performers and performance. The late 1980s ushered in the era of "Just Do It," which was originally associated with Bo Jackson, a superstar American athlete with the unique distinction of receiving All-Star designation for both professional Major League Baseball and professional NFL Football, while impressively also winning the College Football Heisman Trophy and being elected into the College Football Hall of Fame. This tagline, and the campaign cleverly entitled "Bo Knows," allowed Nike cross-training footwear to take off in the marketplace. If Bo knew how great cross-trainers were, certainly the rest of the population could benefit from it.

So as they moved toward the digital transformation era, both Adidas and Nike were in good positions. They had a sound brand strategy, they had loyal followership, and they had innovative products. However, like many brands, they experienced a decline in business as the market began to change and commoditize. Suddenly there were many brands on the market, each with specialty products, distinctive designs, and with unique endorsements that allowed them to capture the attention of the market. Fashion trends emerged quickly and disappeared equally quickly, often with the season but equally often at the whim of various influential celebrities. The decline of Adidas and Nike wasn't exclusively the commoditization of the market – Adidas's early 1990s decline is also attributed to poor management decisions and the death of Adi Dassler's son,[8] while Nike's decline is attributed to a scandal involving manufacturing sweat shops and the slowdown of Asia's economy in the late 1990s[9] – but a contributor to both was the proliferation of brand messages, information, and options available to consumers through these newly emergent digital channels.

Fortunately for both brands, they took a page from their product positioning and never stood still. Both Nike and Adidas recognized the need to redefine their brand strategy and shift to a model that emphasized the experience and not the product. The product, including shoes and other apparel, became the access point to the experience or the output of the experience, but no longer was the driver of engagement and growth.

CREATING AN ENGAGED COMMUNITY

So how did Nike just do it? How did it pivot from product to experience? Nike accomplished this through a series of digital solutions that addressed the ultimate need of its buyers: Get active, stay active, and perform at their highest level of athletic ability, regardless of sport or activity. While Nike products continued to maintain fashion value in their own right, they served a critical function for most buyers, with specialization by sport further reinforcing that function.

Creating the fitness experience for Nike began by creating a community, as most people are social by nature and often are driven by participation and competition, however friendly, with others. Nike established an online presence early, launching Nike.com at the Atlanta Olympics in 1996 with a large media splash seen around the world.[10] They fast followed this launch with the rollout of their first commerce site in 1999, capturing the early online commerce adopter as well as those struggling to find specific products in their local retail store or mall.[11]

They were early entrants to social media platforms as well, participating in some of the first online communities dedicated to topics of fitness and sport. As Nike's Global Digital Brand and Innovation Director, Jesse Stollak, said in an interview with Mashable in 2011, the goal was to gain insight into how the brand connects with fans on a global scale. In the interview, Stollak said that the real focus was about connecting with consumers where they were. "We started with the notion that this was about publishing to them with the right message and at the right time. We've quickly evolved to a focus on conversations and engaging them to participate as opposed to using new media in traditional ways."[12]

Stollak went on to explain that Nike's first foray into social and online communities was launched in 2004, when Nike worked with the media company Gawker to launch "Art of Speed," a series of speed-based short films designed to motivate and inspire consumers.[13] This experiment expanded in partnership with Google in 2006, when Nike launched its Joga campaign and expanded it into the online community. *Joga,* which means "play" in Portuguese, was launched in parallel with the FIFA World Cup in Germany that same year, and was designed to build on the excitement around the worldwide football tournament and emotion that it provoked. It was incredibly forward thinking for its time; it enabled users to create their own profiles, pick their favorite players, choose teams and pitches, post their own photos and videos, and form global social networks with others to share, debate, and celebrate the heart and soul of football.[14]

What's brilliant about this strategy is that it in no way focuses on or emphasizes the Nike products, which would bring the product back into the realm of commoditization. Instead, it creates an emotional connection with the consumer based on the passion for the sport of football, and it extends that connection by allowing individuals to share their passion with people known and unknown across the world on an emerging platform that was building in interest and excitement by the day. The experience was overtaking the product, and it naturally led to loyalty for the brand and its products through that experience. Even more cleverly, the initial rollout was available by invitation only, which created a sense of exclusivity.

This became one of the earliest examples of the power of influencer, or earned, digital marketing, as individuals promoted Joga .com with their friends and family, encouraging others to sign up and participate in the branded community, powered by Nike. This effectively became one of the first social media networks online, during a period when MySpace was just gaining traction and Facebook was limited to university students, capturing over a million online participants. Nike kept them engaged through interactive content, real-time sport updates, and inspired ideas for fitness and activity, which built further connection to the brand in ways that traditional advertising could no longer achieve.

Nike went on to expand the Joga concept, promoting beautiful play and brilliant football while sponsoring local youth tournaments that, according to Nike's own press release in 2006, attracted 3 million players from over 40 countries.[15] Further, they didn't stop there, and continued to press forward with new experiences, leveraging another new and novel platform at the time, YouTube, which had launched the previous year and rapidly increased to a catalog of over 2 million videos by the end of 2005. Video was the perfect medium for a brand like Nike that was looking to inspire activity and action, and Nike was soon posting inspiring content on one of the first branded YouTube channels in history. In fact, Nike holds the honor of posting the first video on YouTube to gain 1 million views,[16] with Brazilian football star Ronaldinho completing a crossbar challenge in Nike cleats. Later websites indicate that the video was actually doctored and therefore fake, but the impact was very real, and the community of Nike fans was expanded.

Given this was a Nike branded video, the argument could be made that this represents a traditional advertising approach, but there's a critical difference that is the essence of this strategy. Content was now being created that individuals willingly accessed and concentrated on, rather than content that was being avoided. This is a key difference between branding experiences versus products. Recall that the Ronaldinho video and the branded YouTube channel were created during the age of TiVo and Digital Video Recording (DVR), allowing consumers to fast forward through the brand commercials when watching events. During a period when consumers were relishing the ability to avoid commercial interruptions, Nike was drawing people to their commercial experiences and building excitement along the way. Nike was aggressive in leveraging new digital experiences as they were introduced, including building communities on Facebook in the United States, QQ in China, Mixt in South Africa, and VKontakte (VK) in Russia. They expanded beyond football, creating dedicated communities for individual sports and activities that expanded their reach and engagement levels further. The strategy worked far beyond their initial expectations, and, by September of 2011, Nike had a dedicated following of over 50 million individuals engaged in their social communities. All these people were proactively engaging with the brand and sharing their ideas, achievements, and questions during a time when people were tuning out and away from traditional brand messages on traditional channels.

Nike took the idea of experiential engagement to another level with the introduction of Nike+ (Nike Plus), which started on a customized iPod device in 2006 and gained steam when introduced for the iPhone and Android devices in 2010. This innovative app experience used early wearable technology (such as a Polar band or a device embedded in the sole of the shoe) and emergent technology on the Apple and Android devices (the GPS on the phone or the Accelerometer on the Nike+ iPod Touch) to track basic fitness information (distance traveled, pace, and calories burned). It rapidly became a community-building experience because Nike offered the ability to sync the device data with the website, which alone encouraged individuals to engage more frequently. Even more effective was the introduction of the forum, which allowed users to post their achievements, challenge one another to fitness activities, and ask questions of other athletes. This form of engagement, known as gamification, kept people both motivated and involved with the brand while equally fusing their desire to interact with digital platforms during this height of the digital transformation era. To be honest, it wasn't perfect, and Nike suffered the negative effect when the application didn't perform to expectations, didn't provide the level of security and privacy that people demanded, and didn't introduce new features at a pace expected by the population of users, but overall it was a positive experience. People continued to "Just Do It," and Nike products retained their popularity and loyal following during this time of product commoditization.

Nike continued to add capabilities, such as engaging an online coach to help train for a marathon or simply find a community of like-minded athletes to remain motivated and engaged during the doldrums of a workout regimen. People would meet online via the Nike forums and then meet in the gym, knowing that they shared a common interest and passion that transcended Nike. As Antonis Kocheilas told me in our conversations, "Nike's ecosystem didn't serve my needs to buy, but they did serve my need to buy into a brand. Once you buy into a brand, you will buy from that brand." That was certainly the case with Nike products throughout the 2000s and into the 2010s.

As the digital transformation era evolved and social communities turned a bit stale, Nike continued to evolve and adjust in response, serving as a true brand pioneer and example of the power of continuous evolution and evaluation. Nike recognized that as the digital transformation wave was starting to crest, consumers were shifting back to a desire for physical experience but one that included digital enablement and integration. In response to this realization, in November of 2016, Nike made yet another splash by opening its flagship experience store in New York's Soho district. As Nike stated in their own words, "Nike Soho – a five-story, multi-sport, 55,000-square-foot retail experience – . . . [is] designed to deliver the best of Nike's personalized services, from exclusive trial spaces to product customization . . . [creating] a seamless link between Nike's digital and physical platforms."[17] Suddenly Nike fans could try out new designs first discovered on digital platforms on the in-store basketball floor, where they'd play a half-court game against Nike employees. Runners can test new shoes on a treadmill while enjoying the countryside of France displayed on a floor-to-ceiling interactive screen. Finally, not to be forgotten, the Nike+ Soccer (Football) trial zone offered synthetic turf and the opportunity to try various Nike soccer cleats in a real environment.

The Nike Experience store took the idea of experience and extended it far beyond a simple trial. Employees became "in-store certified trial athletes" that could help explain product features and benefits while providing an actual competitive situation within which to test the products themselves. The basketball court included high-definition floor to ceiling screens and simulated sound from New York's Washington Heights and Brooklyn Bridge parks, so that the consumer could feel as if they were using the shoes in an actual playground environment playing against some of the great urban hoopers. This was omnichannel experience at a completely different level, and Nike's experience store became a must-see destination for tourists and locals in New York City alike. As a result, the Nike brand continued to grow followership and loyalty, and Nike's revenues continued to increase.

PIVOTING TO GAIN MARKET SHARE

Compared to Nike, Adidas took a slightly more muted tack toward digital transformation. They pursued a route of product innovation and expansion, buying competitive companies including the

Salomon Group (Salomon, Taylor Made, Mavic, and Bonfire) in 1997 and Reebok in 2006. Not to be outdone, the core Adidas team also launched new product features such as ClimaCool in 2002 and adizero in 2004. They rolled out the slogan "Impossible is Nothing" and used brand ambassador David Beckham to reinforce the importance of setting and striving to achieve your personal goals. They introduced Boost technology in 2006 and focused on the basics of selling a quality shoe, allowing the experience of the shoe to be expressed through the buying and ownership experience. They launched their first website in 1997, months after Nike's launch, but unlike Nike they didn't embrace digital experiences as a cornerstone of growth in the same way. They focused on product construction and craftsmanship along with athletic endorsement.

Adidas began communicating a digital strategy publicly in earnest starting in 2015, and at that time there was a clear market share impact, particularly in the United States, where Nike enjoyed 21.1% market share compared to Adidas' 4.7%. Some of that was certainly the result of localization, as Western Europe's 2017 market share was far tighter (10.2% for Nike, 7.8% for Adidas), but the fact that Nike was winning in Adidas' backyard certainly validated the impact of digital transformation on brands.[18] After Adidas adopted their digital strategy in 2015 and began more aggressively investing in digital and social media marketing, Adidas started to grow more quickly (their 2017 year-over-year growth was reported to be over 17.6% for athletic footwear, whereas Nike only grew at 6.8% that same year), but to be fair, at that point Nike's total revenue was 60% more than Adidas, making percentage growth more difficult to achieve for the Portland-based brand.

During the several years before their aggressive adoption of digital, Adidas continued to market the athlete and the association of the product to the athlete, focusing on the vision and desire to replicate the performance of the athlete within the individual. It was a well-executed and well-formed branding strategy, but it was rooted in the past. Up until 2017, when Adidas truly started embracing the foundation of digital marketing and digital experience, Adidas fell behind in market-share and customer loyalty, even though, in the humble opinion of this author and the perception expressed by many experts within the industry, the quality of the product and the level of design innovation was equivalent to that of Nike during the same period. There was no product distinction of note, but Nike was faster in meeting the customer where they were, which was active and embedded in the throes of digital experiences and digital dialogue.

While it's helpful to reflect upon and learn from the many innovative pivots that Nike took as a brand to remain relevant and successful during the period of digital transformation, and reflect on the accelerated brand adoption curve that Adidas captured when they began embracing digital, that's looking to the past. The past is critical to understanding the opportunity of the future, but it's not the path to the future itself. So let's focus on what we can gain and learn from in our current post-digital transformation era. Much of this can be extracted from these lessons and from key steps that both Nike and Adidas are taking to capture market share going forward.

THE FUSION OF DIGITAL AND PHYSICAL PERSONALIZATION

Nike continues to market athletic and overall wellness experiences through investment in the Nike Plus app, which further drives relevance of the brand. As Antonis Kocheilas reminded me, "If customers buy into the brand, they will buy from the brand." Nike Plus allows athletes to not just track workouts and challenges athletes to workout, it now provides far greater engagement and value, creating a wellness experience in its own right. The application ecosystem encourages people to learn, to investigate, and to explore methods for improving their fitness and their performance across a range of sports, from football (soccer) to golf to running. It offers customized workouts based on biometric data, creating the ultimate in customization to the individual. It helps the individual overcome plateaus and reach higher goals. Most importantly, in the post-digital transformation era, it encourages engagement beyond digital, bringing traffic to one of their many branded stores including Nike Outlets, Nike Live, Nike Rise, or – in their largest markets of New York, Paris, and Shanghai – the Nike Innovation Center. Each format leverages the concept of selling experiences over products.

Nike Live is a neighborhood-centric format, creating a sense of intimacy and relevance within the community and fostering the need for community and connection that meets a key emotional and social need. After we all overindexed as societies toward digital, burying our heads in mobile devices, social media feeds, and stream- ing content, most people – with all due to respect to the extreme introverts – have an increased need of human interaction. At the end of the day, we need each other. We need the real-time interaction and physical presence. Digital, for all of its benefits and innovation, only trigger two senses – sight and sound – whereas humans more typically need to use all five to engage. Bringing us back full circle to a physical experience achieves that, and the Nike Plus application encourages people to engage more deeply with the brand through their neighborhood Nike Live store.

The store reflects the neighborhood within which its located, such as the flagship store in the Melrose neighborhood of Los Angeles. Dif- ferent neighborhoods have different needs, different passions, differ- ent activities, and even, at times, different vocabularies, and creating an emotional connection with today's post-digital transformation consumer requires that level of intimate connection in the physical store, because today's consumer is conditioned to intimate personal- ization through the digital channel. Effectively, today's experiences have come full circle, and Nike Live is an effective answer to that need. According to Cara Salpini in a recent Retail Dive post, Nike plans to open over 200 Nike Live stores in the coming months.[19]

Nike Rise is a similar concept to Nike Live but at a larger scale. First opened in Ghangzou China, they recently opened the pinnacle store in Seoul, South Korea. Like Nike Live, the Rise concept is focused on the local area, but that area is more of a city than a neigh- borhood. Further, it is more data-driven than the Live store. By studying the engagement patterns of customers, both online and in-store, within the geography, the Nike Rise store can better predict what will meet the need of the individuals. According to Daniel Heaf, vice president of Nike Direct in 2021, the Nike Rise format creates an individual connection with each customer. The goal is to connect the consumer to their neighborhood and to their city, drawing on the hometown civic price and identity that, in many individuals, evokes a strong emotional connection.[20]

Nike plans to use this data to create tailored experiences relevant to the local resident. For example, Nike Rise stores will have a section of the store labeled The Huddle, where shoppers can sign up for events including wellness discussions with experts, local runs, or fitness classes held locally in the store. Further incorporating lifestyle and fitness into the format, the Nike Rise store sells nutrition and hydration products for pre- or postworkout fueling. Finally, they've installed a Broadcast Booth in The Huddle to hold both virtual and in-person training sessions and events.[21] Effectively, the Nike Rise stores are serving as a gym, a training facility, a social hangout, a nutrition center, and, when needed, an apparel store. The products go virtually unnoticed, eclipsed by the experience itself.

This concept isn't unique to Nike with their store concept. Lululemon has opened "Experiential Megastores" and Dick's has been exploring expanded formats to their flagship store, installing a rock-climbing wall, a turf field, batting cages, and offering personal appointments with wellness experts. In parallel, the retailer is in the process of incorporating more experiential offerings in its full network of stores to address the evolving expectation of the modern athletic consumer.[22] This shift to an experience-led, digitally enabled strategy is paying dividends for all brands.

Adidas is following a similar path, opening new Adidas-branded physical stores complete with unique, individual experiences, but Adidas is more focused on the value of customization and digital-physical fusion of the product design and build process. As Antonis Kocheilas explained to me, "Adidas recognizes that the buying experience has stages — steps in the journey — and Adidas cleverly unlocks certain experiences only after the consumer has bought, which creates the initial commitment to the brand." This isn't abandoning the idea of emphasizing experiences over products; it simply inspires commitment to gain access to the experience. Once the individual has joined the Adidas family, purchasing a product, they gain access to product customization tools that allow collaboration and a sense of uniqueness to the brand.

This approach enhances the value of the experience itself, Antonis went on to explain, because it creates a sense of exclusivity that is a key emotional trigger, similar to how loyalty programs offer elite tiers with level-specific benefits. Not only do certain customers gain access to this collaboration opportunity, they equally gain the opportunity to create a unique product offering for themselves that reflects their personality, sense of style, and individual creativity. Further, Adidas reserves the right to incorporate these ideas into future products themselves, creating a sense of pride and an unparalleled connection with the brand itself. Adidas extends these collaborations to include high-profile celebrities including, in the last half-decade, Pharrell Williams, Kanye West, and Lego. While consumers work through the collaborations and further engage with Adidas at a deeper emotional level, Antonis highlighted, Adidas continues to modify the digital experiences to the individual's experiences, fusing the digital and physical experiences together. It allows individuals to shape the brand based on their individual needs and their individual actions. Adidas is also making early investments in emerging nonfungible tokens, or NFTs, which will allow the consumer to create virtual shoe designs that can be used in the metaverse. That's discussed in Chapter 10, Looking to the Future, along with context on NFTs and the metaverse for those not familiar with the term.

Nike is employing similar personalization strategies in the Nike Rise stores and Innovation Centers. Through the Nike Plus ecosystem, customers can sign up for one-on-styling appointments and workshops, which can be held either in-store or virtually. These sessions focus on five pillars: movement, mindfulness, nutrition, sleep, and recovery.[23] According to Nike's Heaf, styling appointments can provide guidance and advice on which combination of

Nike products, from shorts to running apparel to trainers, will best meet the customer's need based on their activity profile and goals. For the fashion conscious, the Nike Stylist offers recommendations to achieve the latest streetwear look representative of the city. This is the ultimate in personalization, connecting the individual with their brand in the context of their environment.[24]

Nike, like Adidas, has also made recent investments in NFT and metaverse design capabilities, which is also discussed in Chapter 10.

The Nike Rise store, like the Experience Center, is a fluid mix of physical and digital components designed to engage and delight the customer while meeting both known and unmet needs. Standard capabilities like Buy Online, Pickup in Store (BOPIS) digital product reservations, and digital returns have been around for a few years. That's table stakes in the post-digital transformation era.

To access these capabilities, and to access the personalized product section of the store that's the natural output of many of these one-to-one sessions, it's necessary that the customer join the Nike Plus membership program. It's not a requirement, Heaf explains in the Digital Rise article, but it certainly enhances the experience dramatically. Similar in style to Adidas, Nike is building loyalty through engagement, but their method of motivation is different. They are unlocking experiential capability through their digital application and membership program.

Nike, like Adidas, recognizes that the digital–physical fusion is pushing personalization capabilities to another level. In the Nike Rise store, Nike has embedded radio frequency identification (RFID) tags inside the shoes and, when the shoe is set on an RFID-enabled comparison table, the customer sees product details for both the selected the shoe and for other similar designs. They also allow consumers to design their own apparel, such as T-shirts, or collaborate with celebrity Korean designer Jaehoon Choi.[25]

Nike even is enhancing the physical surroundings of the Rise store, first in Seoul, with several large LED screens that respond to movement and draw the individual in. However, the centerpiece of the Seoul store is one central atrium screen they are calling "Sport Pulse," and it's unique to the city. According to Digital Rise, Nike has developed a platform that collects data from Seoul to generate local stories and experiences. This data is collected from Nike's commerce and activity applications, such as Nike+, as well as from local forecasts, teams, and individual athletes.[26] Again, the effect is to create an experience uniquely tailored to the individual in their environment, creating a deeper connection that translates into a stronger emotional bond.

According to Digital Rise, Heaf refers to it as an operating system for the store itself, but it also reflects what Nike is trying to do at scale: Use data to power personalization and build out its ecosystem of store concepts and apps. And, perhaps more importantly, make Nike customers worldwide feel that the retail giant truly knows them, and their specific city.

Heaf goes on to explain in the Digital Rise article that Nike elected to open the first Rise store in Seoul because it is one of the most digitally connected markets, reflecting a trend across broader Asia. However, this trend is rapidly penetrating the globe, particularly with younger generations. Nike, and all brands, need to adopt this strategy in every geography, and every demographic, in order to continue to gain the attention, the commitment, and ultimately the loyalty of the customer. The full circle will complete itself, regardless of industry, and customers will expect a brand to fuse together digital and physical at the points most convenient to the need and to the individual at that moment in time. Financial services brands, hospitality brands, manufacturing brands, all industries – need to embrace this strategy in order to retain the attention and commitment of their customer base.

CUSTOMER CONNECTION, PERSONALIZATION, AND OMNICHANNEL STRATEGY

So what are the critical lessons we can learn from the Nike and Adidas stories? There are three, and these three apply to all brand experiences looking to increase sales, engagement, and volume.

First, it's critical to understand who the customer is and what matters to the customer. While this is a lesson that can be gleaned from the Starbucks story, it's more specific and directive in the Nike and Adidas stories. When experiences are directed at both needs and emotional triggers, the effect on the customer and their progression through the journey accelerates dramatically. Nike and Adidas did this early on by aligning with specific sports and with high-profile athletes in the beginning, each of which had specific sets of participants and, for the most part, a common perspective on what is important to them and what motivates them. As both brands matured into the digital age, they began creating communities such as Nike's Joga, which allowed a direct conduit between the company and the customer and started a dialogue that influenced future offerings. Combined together with improved data and analytics, Nike and Adidas were able to both run market tests to better understand the customer and directly ask the customer what was most important to them.

If your brand doesn't have a similar conduit with your customer, through communities, through social media platforms, through surveys, and through data, it's critical to engage with the customer as soon as possible. Customers are stepping away from brands and are less influenced by brand messaging in the modern era, which means that the opportunities to impress and engage the early-stage customer are reduced, and the opportunities to propel the customer through the engagement and loyalty stages are limited. Every interaction must meet an emotional need, and it's difficult if not impossible to understand those needs without a measured and methodical insight gathering approach.

Second, personalization is key, as it creates an emotional connection that far transcends the emotion generated by the product itself. This includes capabilities far beyond simply recognizing who customers are and presenting their names, favorites, and history when they identify themselves within a channel. When developing the understanding of the customer, focus on the opportunities to speak to each individual as a customer of one and focus on the opportunities to create an experience that speaks to that individual. Adidas focused on platforms that allow the customer to express their unique identity – customization tools and recommendation tools – while Nike built experiences that connect the customer with their environment, their city, and their neighborhood. Both Nike and Adidas allowed the user to progress toward their personal goals by engaging their friends and members of their community in social competition, tracking workouts, posing friendly competitions, and encouraging others to succeed. These applications are fully flexible, allowing the customer to customize their experience, and find their own value, in the Nike and Adidas experience, which creates a deeper sense of loyalty to the brand. There are several opportunities for brands to create emotion-evoking personalization, and it should be a priority to find the opportunity unique to each brand.

Third, leverage digital and data not in isolation, but as part of an integrated omnichannel strategy. Digital should enhance and compliment the physical experience, not replace it. While digital channels can stand on their own – I can order products, I can complete transactions, and I can address an enquiry – the customer shouldn't be limited to the digital channel or view the digital channel as independent of the physical channel. It's critical to recognize that the lessons of this chapter are more than simply adopting an "omnichannel on steroids" experience strategy; neither is it merely extending and enhancing the age-old approach first adopted at the start of the digital era. Instead, as reflected in the Nike and Adidas earlier examples and as reflected by other forward-thinking brands including Uber, Airbnb, and others, the key is that the digital experience is so seamless and deeply integrated that it is invisible. As Antonis Kocheilas cleverly stated to me, "Fish aren't aware of the water, and humans aren't aware of digital. Both just are – they simply exist – and the only time that we notice the absence is when they are absent." The expectation has gone beyond the extreme to the expected, and without it, the brand is bound to fail. Digital is no longer the differentiator, and as Antonis told me, "Talking about digital is simply stupid." Use digital to differentiate your brand experience, while equally adding value by predicting in advance the immediate need of the individual and serving it. Conveniently, that's the topic of the next chapter.

CHAPTER 6

Time Is the New Currency – Anticipating without Being Invasive

Ben Franklin, the source of so many famous quotations, is commonly attributed with first saying that "time is money." Although I freely admit I had never read Franklin's "Advice to a Young Tradesman" before preparing to write this book, I discovered the phrase in that piece. Specifically, Franklin wrote: ". . . Remember that time is money. He that can earn ten shillings a day by his labour, and goes abroad, or sits idle one half of that day, tho' he spends but sixpence during his diversion or idleness, ought not to reckon that the only expense; he has really spent or rather thrown away five shillings besides . . ."[1]

Franklin was reminding this unnamed tradesman that time spent not working is time spent not earning. It's good advice for certain, as it emphasizes the importance of hard work, of focus, and of output. Many sources highlight that this phrase actually goes back to the time of the Greek philosophers, but the essence of the phrase rings true, whether we are talking about the time of Aristotle in the fourth century BCE, the time of Franklin in the eighteenth century, or the modern millennium in the twenty-first century. However, like all great concepts and philosophies, the idea has evolved and morphed to adapt to the reality of today. Today, the focus isn't on spending time working, but instead on being more efficient with time. I refer to this as collapsing time.

COLLAPSING TIME

The advent of digital introduced a new concept that has taken hold and become a critical value – the idea of collapsing time. As members of the modern society, we often talk about how there aren't enough hours in the day, how we never have time for desired activities, how we don't have time to think. This need to be more efficient, to fit in more activity, and ultimately to generate more output, in the same number of hours has been the primary driver of innovation. Products that are truly invisible to us today – the telephone, the automobile, the washing machine, the microwave, the fax machine – are all examples of innovations designed to give time back to the individual by allowing tasks to be performed faster and with less effort. The market positioning may have been convenience, but convenience is primarily a function of time.

Every digital tool has been designed to collapse time in some form, even if it's not the primary value proposition. When Google was first introduced, it saved the time of hunting and pecking for websites. Certainly, it opened up access to sites that otherwise would not have been found, but faster identification and access was a key proposition of web search. Even today, Google proudly displays the time taken to complete the search – when I searched for "Who first said time is the new currency" just now, the top of the results in Google said "About 774,000,000 results (0.63 seconds)." That certainly was much faster than having to drive to the local library, find the encyclopedias, look up the phrase, discover that the phrase isn't in the encyclopedia, and then drive home in frustration, only to open the browser and ultimately find the answer on Google.

As an aside, I likely would have discovered that the last version of the Encyclopedia Britannica was printed in 2010, which very well may have been before this turn of phrase was first coined.

Coming back to the topic, I still don't know who first coined the phrase "time is the new currency," because despite the 774 million results returned by Google, I didn't find an answer to that question. Don't get me wrong; there are many publications and posts that use the phrase. It's just that there's not a single attribution the way that "time is money" is attributed to Ben Franklin (with a nod to Socrates, Plato, and Aristotle). I love the phrase, and have incorporated it into my daily discussion with clients, because it's a pithy way of explaining the value of convenience and acceleration in today's world. Consumers and business customers alike will pay a premium to gain back time, whether that premium be in hard currency or in loyalty to the brand.

As outlined earlier the first example of collapsing time in the Internet era was definitely the web search. Setting aside Yahoo!'s initial directory, the ability to enter a phrase and have a system return relevant results was transformative in the mid-1990s, and remains transformative today. Alphabet, the parent company of Google, built one of the largest businesses in history on this foundation, and while they've diversified their offerings significantly, the foundation of search, and the advertising revenue it generates, remains the primary source of income and growth.

Website design equally focused on the principles of simplicity and intuitive design, finding ways to streamline navigation and guide the individual to find the information, transactional functionality, and other capabilities as quickly and efficiently as possible. A new discipline, digital information architecture, emerged in the early 2000s that was exclusively focused on the art and science of collapsing time. These specialists studied techniques for organizing menus and content that map to the natural thinking of the individual, which allowed people to find what they were looking for more quickly. Efficiency and speed became a measurement of the early websites, and studies were completed demonstrating that if a site wasn't intuitive and quick to navigate, the visitor would quickly abandon it and find another site. The realization that the competition was suddenly a click away took hold, and the race to collapse time while online reached full speed.

Naturally, this quickly led to an evolution in the application of search functionality. Digital designers and architects recognized that search could be as broad as Google or Wikipedia, but it could equally be as specific as searching for words on a website or content on a mobile application. Any functioning digital experience now offers a robust search function, regardless of whether that experience is accessed by a browser, a native app, a gesture, or a person's voice. Further, well-designed digital experiences no longer only present static menus, they now ask the question of "How can I help you today?" using technology known as natural language processing. This saves the time of having to interpret and evaluate a menu and, instead, routes the individual immediately to the function or information required. These few precious seconds make an outsized difference in perception.

Alongside search, the idea of predictive experiences, based on personalization engines, rapidly gained traction across all digital experiences. If the experience recognizes who the individual is and is able to present content and functionality relevant to that individual's needs, wants, and history, the time spent on the current ask will be shorter. As data and analytics technology continue to evolve, now supported by modern artificial intelligence (AI) and machine learning (ML) tools, the ability to create personalized and predictive site experiences continues to improve, and modern digital experiences are far more efficient than those designed just 20 years ago.

However, as with many advancements, this improvement has come with a cost in the form of increased privacy concerns and privacy regulations. As discussed in Chapter 2, The Dawn of Digital, the advancements in personalization and ad targeting ultimately backfired on companies and brands as the perception of invasiveness took hold. Governments have now passed regulatory statutes that limit what data can be captured and shared, and where that data can be stored. There's been quite a bit of press surrounding the "death of the cookie," an initiative led by browser technology companies to block third-party tracking, and sites are already required in major countries to publish their tracking policies. Individuals are demanding anonymity, but that works in reverse to the idea of collapsing time, as an anonymous experience is far less efficient. All this has forced experience teams to change their design paradigms, often encouraging immediate authentication of the visitor and, with that, permission to access their historical data. Once authenticated, brands have more opportunity, and an implied agreement with the customer, to gather relevant and value-added information that allows for a personalized and predictive experience. As this authentication process itself becomes faster and easier, through facial, voice, and touch ID recognition, the value of authentication will again return the value of time.

The evolution of online commerce and fuel that's driven its exponential growth over the last 20 years is the impact of all of the concepts outlined earlier. The idea that the consumer no longer needed to hunt and peck for a specific product was revolutionary when first introduced in the 1990s. There was a novelty element to it in the early days – a brand differentiation we'll explore in Chapter 7, Finding a Novel Approach to Solving a Market Need – but more than that was a time-collapsing element. Prior to online commerce, finding a specific product, whether it was an article of clothing, a popular gift idea, or a replacement part for my car, required that I grab the yellow pages, pick up the phone, and call store after store to find it in stock. That assumes that I'm searching during the days and hours that the store is open, which was limiting in its own right. I then needed to hop in the car, drive to the store, navigate to where the product was being held or on the shelf, buy the product, and drive back home. At that point, I may discover that I got the wrong product – wrong size, wrong color, wrong configuration – and then I needed to start the journey all over again. As we reflect on this history, it sounds absolutely barbaric. If nothing else, it was definitely inefficient. The evolution of commerce, be it the purchase of a physical product, subscription to a service, or engagement for a specific purpose, has now become a fully automated and seamless experience, with functional elements such as transparency, proactive notifications, preemptive processing, and location-based decisioning all helping to collapse time and benefit the customer.

That said, we don't want to exclusively focus on digital. The world and the customer continue to engage across a range of channels. So while the preceding historical review of innovation is exclusively focused on the digital revolution, that does not assume that the only impact is in the digital channel. To the contrary, there are significant opportunities to collapse time during physical engagement, whether it is in person, in store, or on the phone. The data, insights, and automation functionality of digital, in the hands of an employee, partner, or the customer themselves, can increase efficiency and collapse time during a physical interaction. Employee tools can provide data, insights, transactional functionality, and other value-added capabilities in the palms of their hands, delivered via their smart phone, their tablet, or their computer. This physical-digital fusion is accelerating in the post-digital transformation era, and there's quite a bit to learn from forward-thinking companies that are investing across all channels.

This leads us to the brands worthy of study in this chapter: Amazon and Panera Bread. Both have embraced the idea of giving time back to the customer, both have focused on digital transformation and physical-digital multichannel optimization, and both have realized enormous returns as a result.

TIME-SAVING CONVENIENCES

Needless to say, there's quite a bit to learn from Amazon's story, including techniques to employ as you move your brand forward in the post-digital transformation era. Amazon indisputably is the most successful growth story in the history of commerce. In fact, Amazon could be used as an example of a company embracing every recommendation outlined in this book, and through those recommendations it has realized global ubiquity, worldwide loyalty, and exponential growth across every measurable dimension.

Interestingly, Amazon's brand was not always synonymous with online commerce. In fact Amazon's origins were quite humble. This wasn't due to a lack of vision – Bezos's vision was massive and revolutionary from the beginning. However, when he bought the Amazon.com domain and incorporated the company in 1994, no one believed that that his online bookseller would become the largest retailer in the world outside of China.[2] (For those who are curious, the largest retailer in the world as of 2021 is Alibaba, given their dominance in China.) In fact, Amazon wasn't even the first online retailer of books; according to Britannica, Computer Literacy, a Silicon Valley bookstore, began selling books from its inventory to its technically astute customers in 1991.[3] Amazon's vision, however, was unique at the time, as Bezos declared that his new company would ship any title to any reader anywhere in the world.

It was a brilliant ambition, but it does beg the question of why this was even a need or a value proposition. Again, the need and the value proposition, at least partially, comes back to time. While common titles at the time, including those of bestselling 1994 authors such as Mary Higgins Clark or John Grisham, could be found quite easily at brick and mortar stores, more obscure texts and titles were difficult to find. While many bibliophiles and bookworms enjoyed the process of browsing shelves of books in the local bookstore, for many others it was a hassle, and the effort required to find a specific title by a specific author within a massive Barnes & Nobles or Borders bookstore became a painful chore.

From the beginning, Bezos recognized the importance of convenience and the criticality of collapsing time. In a letter to shareholders in 1997, Jeff Bezos was quoted as saying, "Today, online commerce saves customers money and precious time. Tomorrow, through personalization, online commerce will accelerate the very process of discovery."[4] Given that he was quoted as saying this a year before Google came into commercial existence, it does show that he truly was a digital visionary setting the precedence of the age.

Early screen shots of the Amazon.com experience show content that emphasizes the value of Amazon's personal notifications. Why be forced to constantly log onto your computer to confirm whether the new publication has been released or a new product is available, when the website can do it on your behalf? Amazon.com was also one of the first sites to incorporate product search into the home page, so that all you needed to do was type in a title or an author and you'd get a short list of options that likely included what you were looking for. That was revolutionary technology at the time. These early conveniences were clear contributors to the realization of Bezos's strategy to "get big fast" in the 1990s. According to Britannica, "Amazon.com did grow fast, reaching 180,000 customer accounts by December 1996, after its first full year in operation, and less than a year later, in October 1997, it had 1,000,000 customer accounts. Its revenues jumped from $15.7 million in 1996 to $148 million in 1997, followed by $610 million in 1998. Amazon.com's success propelled its founder to become *Time* magazine's 1999 Person of the Year."[5]

Bezos's vision extended far beyond books, remaining grounded on the idea of convenience and time savings in these early days. Amazon launched their Associates program – what we today refer to as an online marketplace – in 1996, which allowed other retailers to market and sell their products on Amazon.com, increasing the level of convenience by modeling Amazon as an online superstore, similar to the approach that made physical megaretailers like Walmart, Target, and the multistore suburban mall footprint dominant in the previous decades. This was an instant success, and by 1998 over 350,000 retailers had signed on to the Associates program. Just as these physical models allowed the customer to make one trip in the car to find multiple products, Amazon's Associates program allowed people to search one URL and find multiple products beyond books. First it was music and videos, both shipped to the home on CD/DVDs, and eventually a full range of products.

Amazon was relentless in its focus on saving time and introducing conveniences. In 1999 they introduced the idea of one-click purchasing, allowing customers to enter and save their shipping and payment information for future purchases. This, together with the Amazon account data collected during account creation, allowed Amazon to start collecting browsing and purchasing habits, using that data to create a more personalized, convenient, and streamlined shopping experience.

They set the standard for every other commerce experience, and differentiated their brand by collapsing time.

DATA-DRIVEN INNOVATIONS

Data became the foundation for Amazon's next stage in digital evolution, which changed the overall approach to engagement and experience. Amazon recognized early in the digital transformation era the importance of customer data in developing a personalized experience that will benefit the consumer. If the site can predict what the customer is looking for before the person arrives at the site, the quality of the experience will be far better. As Leah Retta so eloquently stated in her insightful e-book, *AMAZON: The Chronicles of a Personalization Giant*, the "foresight and understanding of the correlation between a shopper's unique needs and the decision-making process would later become critical to what we now know and refer to as the customer experience. A new competitive battleground for brands looking to forge meaningful relationships with customers who have more options available to them than ever before, Amazon has achieved what everyone in the personalization game has hoped to – the ability to create tailored, online experiences designed for specific users that not only reflect a customer's tastes and preferences, but also anticipates their needs."[6]

The key concept here, in terms of the lessons of this chapter, is "anticipation." Using data to profile behaviors and, in turn, using that insight to personalize the interface to anticipated needs, allows the consumer to complete their transaction more quickly, combining together that which they planned to purchase with, potentially, that which they hadn't planned to purchase. Patented in 2001 and rolled out in 2003, this recommendation engine was the ultimate in convenience, effectively putting products together on the virtual shelf, not forcing the consumer to manually search for every product.

The elegance of the recommendation engine, even in its earliest form, was impressive. Amazon used several elements when generating recommendations, ranging from recent purchases made (for known customers) to the geographic location of the browser to purchases other customers have made after buying the current product being viewed. Amazon was careful with their vocabulary, offering a level of transparency to show how they were generating recommendations, keeping the "creepiness factor" at bay while delivering the personalized experience. While there are many angles to explore and unpack in terms of the impact that personalization drove for Amazon, not the least of which is an increased cart size and increased share of customer wallet, for purposes of this discussion it also increased convenience, which drew customers to and kept customers on their site. Over time, this also increased loyalty. Why fight through clumsy, unpersonalized experienced on other sites when Amazon makes it so easy and quick? The more the individual engaged with Amazon, the more that Amazon reflected the unique and specific interests of that individual. The experience became easier and faster with each interaction, encouraging new interactions. It created a brilliant engagement cycle, and Amazon's meteoric rise continued.

By 2004, Amazon started to look like the site that we know today. They were selling a range of products including housewares, electronics, apparel, toys and games, and others. Most notably, they added their A9 search engine, which used keyword tags and other techniques to predict what the visitor was searching for and attempting to present products that most likely represent the search. In 2006, Prime memberships brought two-day shipping, further collapsing the physical time necessary to receive the product but equally importantly, removing the step of having to evaluate different shipping providers, timetables, and costs. Suddenly, the buying process was a click or two less. Over time, that evolved into one-day shipping and eventually same-day shipping in certain markets, sometimes within the hour. Now the online experience could require less time to fulfill than the physical experience, which is truly revolutionary, and again created a superior experience that led shoppers to adopt Amazon.

Amazon continued to introduce data-driven innovations, finding opportunities to exchange convenience and time for the right to collect information about the consumer's behaviors. The data would further improve the convenience, and it became a rapidly accelerating cycle. Amazon created a gift finder that reduces browsing time and helps select the ideal gift for a specific individual and occasion based on the individual and occasion itself. This is a data-driven algorithm that gets smarter with each interaction. They introduced a product-comparison widget that simplifies the process of comparison shopping, without forcing the consumer to run multiple searches to identify and explore competitive products. They added customer reviews that allow for instant validation of both benefits and concerns, which increases the credibility of each purchase decision while using analytics to strategically present the right reviews without falsely suppressing potentially negative ones. Once a product was purchased, Amazon equally simplified the tracking process – sending updates directly to the customer's e-mail, phone, Echo device, or mobile application. The buyer didn't need to go through the steps of tracking a package or even pulling up the order. Instead, order status was sent to the individual. Finally, Amazon recognized that online purchasing would lead to returns, so they built integrated return merchandise authorization (RMA) processes into the site and the app, and buyers – particularly Prime Members – could quickly print return labels and easily return products that didn't meet their exact expectations. Returning on Amazon was a faster and easier experience than returning to a physical store, and the consumer wasn't forced to negotiate a return-to-form-of-payment versus store credit. All these innovations, empowered and improved by data and analytics, collapsed the amount of time required to browse, explore, inspire, evaluate, purchase, track, and return products.

Amazon didn't stop with the on-site experience. They embedded the same functionality into their mobile applications so that Amazon shopping functionality was carried around in the consumer's pocket. This eliminated the need to write down and refer to a separate list. They introduced their Echo device, commercializing the conversational interface, and included a range of time-saving features that were integrated into Amazon shopping, such as the ability to shout across the kitchen while looking in the refrigerator. This reduced the time, and increased the convenience, of the Amazon experience, which was extended when the Echo device began proactively offering to ship replacement products to the house once patterns of usage were detected. The consumer no longer needed to check if they were running low on paper towels, because Amazon began predicting that they needed a restock.

Eventually Amazon introduced grocery delivery, seven-day delivery service, and Amazon Key service. The last offering was perhaps one of the most innovative time-saving services, as it allows the Amazon delivery driver direct access to the consumer's door – either a house door or a garage door – so that the consumer doesn't need to be inconvenienced by waiting for a delivery or worrying about redirection options.

Amazon, perhaps most notably of all, had embraced a physical footprint. Through the acquisition of Whole Foods and through their private branded Amazon stores: Amazon Go Grocery, Amazon Go cashierless convenience stores, Amazon Pop Up themed kiosks, Amazon Books bookstores, Amazon 4-star general merchandise stores, Amazon Fresh Pickup, and an Amazon-branded grocery store planned for Los Angeles, they are clearly experimenting with combinations of physical and digital combinations that will expand both customer share-of-wallet and, equally, increase customer loyalty. Their timing of much of this was unfortunate – right before the COVID lockdowns in 2020 that led to a short-term retail apocalypse – but Amazon had the capital to be able to experiment in any environment. What's most interesting about many of these formats is that they're designed for convenience along with access. For immediate gratification and fulfillment, the consumer could place the order on the application and then pick it up immediately at one of the stores. This has proven particularly popular for subjective selections such as fresh grocery items, where many consumers aren't comfortable with having a third-party picking their fruits, vegetables, and meats. This is now setting a new standard for physical shopping convenience, and other retailers are working actively to catch up.

Amazon's continued use of data to personalize the experience and anticipate needs are truly notable and established a standard of expectation that has penetrated the consciousness of today's generations. If your brand sells products or services online and you haven't adopted the fundamental standards of personalization and anticipation to reduce the time necessary to complete a task, I'm not going to sugarcoat the reality: you're far behind the curve. Fortunately, most brands have adopted this capability, quite often by platforming their commerce on Amazon through their modern marketplace offering and many integrated partnerships.

What has been the impact of this innovation and focus on customer convenience? The end results speak for themselves. With a $1.7 trillion market capitalization as of 2021 and $386 billion in revenue reported at the close of 2020, Amazon would be the twelfth largest economy if ranked against sovereign GDPs. Much of this revenue can be attributed to product innovation, including the wildly popular Amazon Web Services and the extended Amazon Prime suite of services, which include Prime Video and Prime Music, but at their core, it's Amazon's data driven, personalization-centric time collapsing commerce experience that drives the core of its revenue.

MAKING QUICK SERVICE QUICKER

Now let's pivot to a slightly less scaled but equally innovative experience-centric brand in Panera Bread. Panera Bread has always recognized the importance of experience in defining the brand proposition. As articulated by an eTail blog post (the author is not named), Panera adopted a strategy in 2010 they called Panera Warmth. This strategy was based on CEO Ron Shaich's recognition that the Panera Bread brand was being tarnished by the lunchtime line, which forced customers to wait during peak periods.[7] Nothing is more frustrating than having to wait in line for a quick-service experience, and it quickly creates a negative reflection on the brand.

For those readers who do not know the history of Quick Service Restaurant (QSR) operational models, the idea of speed – of collapsing time – certainly predates digital. With 75% of QSR orders consumed outside of the restaurant, there has long been a focus on how to improve the takeaway experience. This led McDonald's to introduce the first drive-through window in 1975, near a military base in Arizona,[8] and a long list of other innovations ever since. Even today, 70% of QSR orders are picked up and taken away, often but not exclusively through the drive-through window. Given this, digital technology was an ideal solution for QSR efficiency, but, interestingly, many QSR brands were relatively slow to adopt digital. Panera Bread saw an opportunity to distinguish their brand.

In 2010, when CEO Ron Shaich first realized that Panera Bread had a challenge with the length of the lunch line and the associated wait time, Panera began investing in their digital experience and opportunities to reduce the amount of time required to patronize their restaurant and, ultimately, enjoy their meal. He used his personal experience to help define their strategy. According to *Fortune* magazine, Ron Shaich frequented Panera for both breakfast and lunch while shuttling his son to and from school. Given he was a busy CEO, he was often running behind schedule, so he would call the restaurant and pre-order his meal. Schaich would drive up and have his son run in with the credit card, skipping the line, and getting them out in a couple minutes. "That was a lovely system except it only worked for the CEO," Shaich said."[9]

Recognizing this problem, Panera Bread implemented a new system that was innovative for the time. It was not exclusively digital, but actually a combined digital-physical experience. Customers could order online, via the web or their mobile device, with full configuration capability available as if the order were placed at the counter. Customers could use the emergent GPS capabilities on the mobile device not just to order lunch but order lunch from the location most convenient to where they are at that moment in time. The order could be prescheduled, allowing the customer to define what time they want to pick it up. This meets the critical need of allowing the customer to control the experience and the timing. These digital advancements, which are relatively commonplace today, were bold steps forward at the time. They addressed Shaich's vision of giving the CEO convenience to every customer.

As mentioned earlier, the new system wasn't only focused on digital or order placement. Order transparency – order status updates – was available both online and in store. There was no need for the customer to take up valuable time inquiring about when their order would be ready. Once the order was prepared, it was put onto a shelf with a clearly printed tag that had the customer's name (or nickname), so the customer didn't even need to interact with an employee if they didn't desire. Further, the mobile application or website identified which shelf the order was placed on. It was the ultimate in real-time convenience.

In full disclosure, I've used this feature countless times to grab-and-go lunch while on a conference call. I didn't even need to mute the conversation to speak with an employee; I could just grab the bag and run back to my office. I'm a personal example of the loyalty and repeat behavior that this system fostered.

This was not a static initiative for Panera Bread, either. Like Amazon, they recognized the opportunity to leverage customer data to improve the experience. Fortunately, they had access to a rich trove of customer information collected, voluntarily and openly, through their loyalty program. To appreciate this, it's important to understand that the QSR customer journey is a bit truncated, typically ending at the point of initial fulfillment. It's a rare occurrence that I'm going to begin an RMA process for my Big Mac or my chicken burrito. However, as with all customer journeys, loyalty remains a strategic goal, typically driven through incentives and, more recently, convenience. Panera Bread followed the pattern of other great loyalty-centric brands such as Subway in providing incentives and earnings to encourage repeat visits, but also early on recognized the value of the loyalty program's inherent data collection and the opportunity to use that data to extend further conveniences to the customer. This new release was named Panera Bread Digital 2.0.

As *Fortune* magazine outlined in their article after Panera Bread's initial Digital 2.0 launch, the application and supporting ecosystem were all about timesaving convenience. Leveraging the MyPanera reward program data, the application would present previous orders and favorite products once the customer identifies themselves at the kiosk. Further, if the customer customizes their order in a new way, this change is captured and available the next time. The customer doesn't need to re-input their unique order with each visit, saving time and building a sense of digital intimacy. Effectively, this new system became the digital equivalent of walking into your favorite diner and telling the waitress that you'll have the usual.[10]

However, it goes beyond the convenience of reorder. Shaich explained at the time that Panera 2.0 was an investment in both customer service and operational improvement. He recognized that while the time-saving convenience of mobile payments and data-driven personalization was notable and compelling to the Panera customer, the long-term benefits were more wide ranging, reducing the wait times in the stores, improving order accuracy, and eliminating crowding around the order counter.[11] All these points align the experience with time and with convenience, while generally propelling the Panera Warmth brand proposition.

Panera didn't stop innovating with the introduction of Digital 2.0. They were also one of the first brands to adopt digital delivery,[12] in 2016, offering the service before it became dominated by delivery aggregation services. This took convenience to another level during a time that delivery was almost exclusively the domain of pizza and Chinese restaurant formats. This offered more insight into the customer, as patterns could be created based on geographies and order patterns to the office and to the home. It was a short-lived program, replaced by agreements with the delivery aggregators in 2018, but it was notable in extending brand value and loyalty.

Finally, Panera extended the digital experience into the store, offering both impulse and augmentation offerings to increase the ticket size while still streamlining the customer journey. Customers didn't need to reestablish their order or even work to identify themselves. Instead, they simply needed to either swipe their MyPanera loyalty card or enter their phone number in the kiosk, and they could instantly modify their order if an impulse triggered them in the store.

POST-DIGITAL DATA AND LOYALTY

Like Amazon, Panera is an organization that doesn't stand still. They are already planning for the post-digital transformation era with their latest "store of the future" concept, integrating the digital and physical experiences to marry together their brand proposition of quality food products and the ultimate in customer convenience. As Eduardo Luz, Chief Brand and Concept Officer for Panera Bread, said to *Hospitality Technology* in 2021, "Innovation is core to who we are and with our new next-generation Panera concept, we are doing what we've always done – keeping a personalized experience for the guest at the heart of everything we do."[13] This bears all the elements of Panera's next-gen store focus on making the customer experience more convenient, reducing the time of each transaction, even if only by seconds. Panera is introducing dual drive-through lanes with a dedicated rapid pickup lane, dedicating space in the drive-through to digital ordering and furthering the physical–digital fusion. They are enhancing their digital experience with contactless dine-in and delivery, a top priority during the COVID pandemic but very likely a continued priority moving forward. The experience will include full contactless ordering via the mobile device either in store, for rapid pickup, or from the drive-through lane, and then contactless through the preparation process, with notifications, receipts, and all other information being provided via the individual's mobile device. The customer doesn't have to interact with or touch anything touched by another person, which is becoming a critical component of the physical experience coming out of the COVID pandemic. This is being provided to address an acute customer need, but it's being designed with the recognition that time is currency. Panera doesn't need to discount their menu to entice the customer in; Panera makes it easy to order and pick up with the confidence of contactless delivery.

Panera's next-generation strategy maintains focus on data and loyalty as well. As Luz outlines to *Hospitality Technology,* they used restaurant foot traffic data to create a design that simplified the guest journey while keeping it compelling. The sights and smells of the bakery were an important part of the restaurant experience, the ordering process was made simple and intuitive, regardless of whether the order was placed at the counter or via a digital kiosk, and the location of food pickup was clearly labeled and located in an area where congregating was comfortable and possible.[14] This is a clever use of data to improve the experience. It subtly enables the customer to navigate the restaurant more quickly, while also helping them move about more comfortably, creating an even more satisfying experience. At the same time, it can also be used to improve in-store operations, creating conveniences that improve the guest experience. That said, Panera continues to use data to directly improve the customer experience and customer convenience, with the next-generation strategy including digital improvement that further integrates loyalty-program data and functionality, allowing customers to save favorites, earn and track rewards, and receive one-to-one content that is customized based on their visit and buying patterns.

This strategy has generated enormous returns over the years. From 1987 to 2017, at which point Panera was sold to JAB Holding Company and taken private, Panera Bread was the highest-performance stock in the restaurant sector. They successfully navigated the COVID pandemic, maintaining their brand image and revenues during the most difficult period for the industry, and they maintained the loyalty of a fan base throughout the many shifts and challenges of the last two decades, ranging from digital threats to new formats to changing customer behaviors. If you're looking for me, there's a good chance that I'll be running through a Panera Bread store picking up my contactless order while participating in a conference call.

FOUR TIME-BASED LESSONS

So what can you learn from Amazon and Panera Bread as you consider your brand experience strategy for the post-digital transformation era? Ultimately, there are four critical lessons tied to the theme of this chapter.

The first lesson is to continuously recognize and explore the opportunities to collapse time. Amazon and Panera Bread's stories show that the real value is generated when you think more innovatively about how to collapse time at every stage of the customer journey. Break it down, as both Amazon and Panera Bread have, to the specific stages of engagement, which will be unique to your individual brand. For example, if customers engage with your brand to sign up for a service, think about the opportunities to reduce the amount of time necessary to find, to explore, to compare, and ultimately to commit to your service. If your brand provides multiple options, present options based on similar visitors – where they are, how they got there, what they've looked at before. Data and analytics can and will open up new opportunities for improvement, decompose every stage in the customer journey, from initial awareness through to loyalty, and evaluate how data can be used to personalize and streamline the experience. Think creatively, and don't be afraid to experiment. As digital has moved from a differentiator to an expectation, experimentation is even more tolerated, and if an approach isn't generating the results that you expect for your brand, tear it down and try another approach. The only thing to avoid is doing nothing. In the post-digital transformation era, the moment your brand stops innovating is the moment that your brand starts declining.

Second, be transparent with the use of data. Both of these brand stories clearly demonstrate the value of first-party data, and with the death of the cookie, there's a sudden focus on first-party data collection. This data can be powerful, particularly when filtered through an analytics engine and used to anticipate needs or generate insights. While you need to collect and leverage it, don't hide the fact that, as a brand, you're leveraging data to improve the experience. Establish a value construct with the customer, using time as a key component of value, which encourages customers to agree to share their information. This was part of both Panera's and Amazon's strategy and core to their collective success. The cleverness of their algorithms extended too far from time to time – there's a prevailing and erroneous belief that Amazon's Echo devices listen to conversations and that Amazon uses that data to suggest products, for example – but overall Amazon has been very effective in their transparency, and they haven't been painted by the media or the masses with the conspiratorial brush that has plagued the other FAANG (Facebook, Amazon, Apple, Netflix, Google) companies. Instead, Amazon embraced transparency, embedding data-driven capabilities into their experience messaging with labels such as "Customers who looked at this product also bought" and "Based on your purchasing history, you may also like." Amazon doesn't hide the fact that they profile using data, but the transparency strips away the creepiness factor of interacting with a site that knows so much about you and your shopping habits. This drives the perfect balance that today's Millennials and Generation Z are demanding of privacy and personalization, ultimately culminating in seamless convenience.

Third, extend the convenience to omnichannel, if physical experiences are part of your customer journey. As we have moved from the digital to the post-digital transformation era, customers – both B2C and B2B – are rediscovering the value of physical interaction and physical engagement. Whether it is driven by the desire for social interaction that was highlighted during the years of the COVID pandemic lockdowns – the need to see, smell, and touch the products being evaluated, or the desire to have a complex, multidimensional evaluative conversation with an expert – generations are rediscovering the physical world, but they're doing it in different ways than before. Panera's approach to physical–digital fusion is notable and pronounced, reflecting the criticality of physical experience in the restaurant industry but, equally, it reflects the shift in behavior by the consumer back to the physical. Amazon's rollout of physical stores is at least in part in response to consumer's need for multisensory evaluation, direct selection, and immediate gratification. Consumers aren't returning to the pre-digital dark age; they are expecting that the physical experience will build off of their digital interactions. They expect to step into the clothing retailer and have their selected items set aside and staged in a dressing room so that they can quickly try them on and assess the fit on their body. They expect that the automotive seller has the vehicle ready for them to complete their test drive. They expect the financial institution to pick up the transaction from the specific point that the customer stopped engaging digitally, and they expect the healthcare provider to have immediate access to the biometric data collected by the wearable that first noted an issue or anomaly. Consumers expect to check in online to their flight, their hotel, and even to their restaurant. This extends to B2B transactions as well; the B2B salesperson hasn't disappeared, but the purchasing customer expects the salesperson to have full awareness of all evaluation activity and configuration data that was completed on digital platforms and to pick up from that point. Again, it's all about time – having to repeat steps, having to backtrack, having to complete tasks that were previously initiated online – this is no longer tolerated and will lead to immediate defection. It's critical to look across every stage of the journey and ensure that complete convenience optimization is incorporated.

Finally, don't hesitate to trade time for money. This is the essence of the phrase "time is the new currency," and the modern interpretation of Ben Franklin's original adage. The convenience of collapsed time within the brand experience drives more than just engagement and loyalty; people are willing to spend more to gain time back. Panera isn't fighting the competitive battle on the pricing front the way that many QSR brands do with dollar menus and upsizing bundles, but instead holds to a premium price construct for quality products served via a convenient experience. Amazon has proved this quite often with commodities that could be purchased elsewhere. Rather than having to click off of Amazon.com and engage with a different site, including but certainly not limited to the equally impressive and scaled Walmart.com, to save a certain percentage, they will remain on the Amazon site and pay the premium. The savings in cost does not justify the additional time investment. This has been proven with inexpensive commodity items but equally with more expensive items, particularly as the consumer considers the entirety of the journey including convenience of fulfillment, convenience of service, and convenience of returns. Amazon has continuously used this principle to drive both revenue and margin on products, and it's an advantage for your brand as well. As we move further into the 2020 decade, the value of time is set to increase further, and savvy brands will cash in on this trend.

CHAPTER 7

Finding a Novel Approach to Solving a Market Need

Redefining an offering or solution is an often-overlooked strategy for capturing brand recognition, engagement, and market share. It's long been known that people are drawn to new things. It's entertaining, it's a break from routines, and it stimulates the imagination. Neuroscience backs this up, with theories ranging from the belief that new things stimulate the fight-or-flight reflex to the more basic belief that modern humans are overstimulated and, therefore, easily bored. Bringing something new to the market, and to your experience, is a powerful tool, when employed properly, to increase engagement and distinguish the brand.

History is filled with examples of revolutionary thinking changing how society as a whole addressed common challenges, starting with hunter-gatherer tools, moving to the invention of the wheel, and continuing forward through various ages of innovation and technological progress. Fortunately, we don't need to reconstruct the entire evolution of innovation across the centuries in order to explore this opportunity, as exciting a prospect as that is. We can focus instead on a few modern examples to extract key lessons that can help you rethink your brand experience strategy through the lens of innovation and novelty.

It's important to remember that *novel* does not mean "radical." While there are multiple examples of radical innovation reflected in this text already, including the automobile, the touch-based smartphone, the Internet, and even the digital revolution as a concept, these are big, broad, society-changing transformations, and therefore not actionable or practical for most brands. Unless your brand has the resources and capital of Amazon, Tesla, or a select list of other highly capitalized companies with significant cash on the balance sheet, the idea of re-imagining something of this scope is, of course, unrealistic and ill-advised. We can learn from these revolutionary events, and we can embrace them as we've embraced digital transformation, but most individual brands aren't going to launch the next worldwide shift.

Equally, there are many examples of what happens when a brand fails to innovate or respond to the shifting needs of their market and their customer. One widely known example is Kodak. It's devastating to consider the path that Kodak took and the rapidity of their decline. An amazing brand headquartered in an equally amazing city, Rochester, New York, both felt the sudden shock of technological disruption and unforeseen adoption of alternative approaches.

Other examples include the taxi industry as a general construct, which was upended by the Uber revolution, and Blockbuster Video, the ubiquitous retail video rental shop in the United States and other countries, that failed to see the impact of the impending Netflix disruption. There are other examples, of course, but the overall lesson is clear – in today's disruption-oriented business environment, standing still is not an option.

The key for most organizations is finding the novel middle ground. This means discovering the opportunity to innovate, surprise, and delight without reestablishing your entire business model. Fortunately, there are plenty of opportunities to augment your brand's approach to marketing, sales, and service to grab the attention, the engagement, and ultimately the commitment of the marketplace. Savvy brands saw this opportunity at the start of the digital transformation era, employing online commerce before others adopted it in earnest; this was the foundation of Amazon's path to success, as discussed in the previous chapter. Other novel capabilities, such as integrating location services and mobile notifications to communicate with consumers when they entered the proximity of a physical location, deploying AI-enabled chat communications, implementing Augmented Reality-enabled experiences, and integrating social communications into the engagement cycle. Brands including PayPal, Peloton, Tesla, Amazon, Dell, Walmart, Starwood (now Marriott), and Domino's are examples of brands that embraced digital innovation early. An entire book could be filled with these examples, and given the speed of recent innovation, there's arguably as many innovation examples during the digital transformation era as there were in multiple centuries prior. The cost, time, and complexity required to create novel experiences has declined substantially in the past 25 years.

That said, there are a few examples that truly stand out for their continuous incremental innovation and recognition of the impact of this ongoing evolution. One highly appealing brand to highlight is Lululemon, the premium athletic apparel manufacturer and retailer with an interesting, and at times tumultuous, history. Let's break their history down a bit, highlighting key lessons from their journey, which conveniently spans the digital transformation era.

AMBASSADORS OF INNOVATION

Lululemon was first founded in 1998, which in itself is a bit surprising given how ubiquitous the clothing, and the brand, are within the markets that they operate. Understanding that their target market is somewhat affluent, the recognizable A logo within the circle is a mainstay in those communities. However, like many of the brands that we highlight in this book, Lululemon's origins were far more humble.

Chip Wilson, the founder of Lululemon, was inspired to start a company after having attended a yoga class in Vancouver, British Columbia. An aficionado of technical athletic clothing design from his 20 years in the snowboard, skate, and surf business, he observed that the cotton apparel that yoga participants wore was both impractical and inappropriate. In Wilson's view, yoga movements required apparel that had flexibility, breathability, and stretchiness, allowing a person to properly sweat while exercising. To address this need, he built a design studio to realize this vision, but, struggling with rent, he converted the studio into a yoga studio in the evenings.[1]

As an interesting aside, the Lululemon name was chosen out of 20 brand names, and the logo is a stylized A, meant to reference the phrase "Athletically Hip." I have to be honest that for years I thought the symbol was a Greek Omega symbol, and it was only recently that I was corrected and told that it was in fact a stylized A. That's not a knock on the logo, but instead a reflection on my poor powers of observation.

From the beginning, Wilson employed an innovative technique that eventually became a mainstay approach across industries: employing influencers to promote the brand. To be clear, I'm not suggesting that Lululemon was the first to do this – brands have been leveraging celebrities in marketing campaigns for decades – but the localization of Lululemon's approach was quite distinctive. Lululemon's original vision for their store was "to create more than a place where people could get gear to sweat in, we wanted to create a community hub where people could learn and discuss the physical aspects of healthy living, mindfulness and living a life of possibility. It was also important for us to create real relationships with our guests and understand what they were passionate about, how they liked to sweat and help them celebrate their goals."[2] From the very beginning, Wilson encouraged the yoga instructors and participants in classes to wear his designs and provide real-time feedback on the quality, effectiveness, and comfort of his designs. This approach became a foundation of Lululemon's influencer strategy.

Lululemon opened their first store in November of 2000 in the beach area of Vancouver called Kitsilano. The fledgling organization quickly realized that they couldn't both serve as a community hub and succeed as a retailer, so they shifted the business. They focused on retailers and concentrated on training the "educator" on the unique and distinguishing characteristics of the products.

For the better part of the early years, Lululemon focused on fundamental retail growth tactics, expanding their product line beyond the initial set of women's yoga pants, expanding the number of retail locations, and establishing a brand identify of Athleisure that extends the fashion of Lululemon to the street. By 2006, Lululemon had opened 27 stores in Canada and another 9 in the United States. Revenue had topped $120 million, and Lululemon had begun developing a cult following, not exclusively because of the technical characteristics of the clothing but also because of the product's ability to flatter the shape of the wearer. Amazingly, they drove this growth without advertising; they didn't have television commercials, radio ads, or newspaper campaigns. They also hadn't yet embraced the digital revolution.[3] Instead, they drove brand awareness through word of mouth and a uniquely designed Ambassador program.

What made Lululemon's Ambassador influencer campaign unique was that, instead of employing celebrity endorsements, their ambassadors were everyday people – yoga teachers, fitness instructors, and similar profiles – who were given free products to wear in return for spreading the word about Lululemon. The Ambassadors were affiliated with local stores that were designed to reflect both the mission of Lululemon and the community within which the store resided. Stores had warm and inviting storefronts that reflected the street and community culture, and the interior design was built to promote engagement, discussion, education, and exploration. Like Starbucks, who employed a similar community strategy, as outlined in Chapter 4, Believing in Your Brand and Redefining Your Strategy, Lululemon was building an emotional connection with women that went beyond the product and even the brand – it was a connection with the vision and the lifestyle that Lululemon represented. Local stores were encouraged to hold events that were relevant to their communities, such as the Santa Monica store which held yoga classes on the beach. Those classes were, as you might expect, led by Ambassadors and replete in Lululemon gear. While a common approach today, at the time, the Ambassador program was quite revolutionary. Lululemon recognized the power of community-centric marketing and brand building, creating a brand that was fueled by the experience – the experience of wearing the product, being active, and focusing on well-being. Today, the Ambassador program, still going strong, includes over 1,500 participants in communities across the globe.

STRATEGIC INNOVATIONS IN CRM

Lululemon didn't stop there. After going public in 2007 and continuing their growth – during the next five years they would open over 100 new stores, expand internationally beyond North America, cross $1 billion in revenue in 2010, and introduce a menswear line in 2014 – Lululemon started to aggressively build on the digital experience and digital opportunity. They launched their first e-commerce experience in 2009. It's easy to appreciate that this would have required significant effort to replicate the value and the connection created by the educators and ambassadors in the store. Lululemon recognized, through this journey, that they needed to create the same personalized experience online, and they launched an aggressive customer relationship management (CRM) initiative to build an e-mail database that would facilitate an interactive dialogue similar to what customers enjoyed in the store. This was a novel approach to online commerce during a time that the majority of retail brands were racing to build and launch standard commerce functionality: category pages, product detail pages, and shopping cart checkout pages. The approach was cleverly grounded in their strategy of maintaining an intimate connection between the educator, the ambassador, and the customer, recognizing that the medium of conversation was shifting from exclusively in-store to a combination of in-store and digital.

Lululemon's approach, as articulated by the EVP of Digital, Miguel Almeida, was cross-platform. They redesigned their website to "make the overall customer experience more cohesive and enjoyable, while investing significantly in building our CRM and analytics capability . . . to really deliver contextually relevant experiences to our guests that bring the story telling of our product and brands . . . connect[ing] those guests back with our stores as well."[4] This aligns with the lessons outlined in Chapter 6, Time Is the New Currency – Anticipating without Being Invasive, on the criticality of data collection and the value that that data can provide in terms of hyperpersonalized experiences, particularly across channels. Almeida continued to roll out new digital initiatives, many focusing on convenience and collapsing time as outlined in Chapter 6, but equally focusing on novelty innovation that, in its own right, drew attention and engagement from consumers curious to try new functionality. An emerging capability that Ameida highlighted in a 2015 interview was BOPIS, or buy online, pick up in store. A new capability at that time, it allowed customers to take advantage of the simplicity and ubiquity of online shopping while still gaining the somewhat immediate gratification of quick fulfillment. This often could be extended, with the educator preparing products that complemented the purchase or even making suggestions based on data from the consumer's profile and buying habits, which becomes a value-added way to increase the transaction value and overall share of wallet of that consumer.

It's important to note that Lululemon didn't abandon their focus on in-store experience that defined their brand. In fact, in 2014, they rolled out a new concept store in Edmonton that addressed a trend at that time toward retail space acting as a "hangout." As outlined in a *Retail Insider* article, Lululemon created a new store design with modifiable common areas that allowed for collaboration, socialization, and even a place to work. Located on Whyte Avenue in Edmonton, the store was designed based on feedback from locals, again aligning to the wants and needs of the unique community, building deeper connection. According to the *Retail Insider* article that was written at the time of the store's opening, the store was filled with people meditating and participating in yoga classes. There were floor mats in place around the store, but there was one woman who was meditating on a table. It was described as quite an eclectic scene, but the article does note that the cash registers were busy, and people were buying a significant number of products even though much of the store wasn't dedicated to retail.[5] Clearly, the store had the desired effect, and again the novelty of the store format drove significant press and equally significant customer engagement.

Lululemon continued to create experiences that engaged the local community, including a pop-up retail area where local vendors could sell products that aligned with the Lululemon experience and brand. Retail expert Bridget Russo was cited in the article, explaining that the alternative-use space in the store motivated people to visit, particularly when the space was used for community meetings and in-store events. It kept the store bustling with customers, built the Lululemon brand as a Main-Street retail supporter, and motivated people to come into a physical store during a time that online commerce was exploding.[6] This is a brilliant example of leveraging novel innovation in experience to further the brand connection and inspire deeper levels of customer engagement, commitment, and loyalty.

Not every innovation proved successful, which is a sign of a well-run innovation function. Fundamentally, innovation teams cannot fear failure, and occasionally, initiatives don't drive return on investment (ROI) as expected. Without exploration, great ideas rarely come to fruition. For example, in 2016, Lululemon opened Lululemon Lab in New York (following up on the original Lululemon Lab concept in Vancouver, which launched in 2009), fusing their store concept with an in-store design incubator, featuring limited edition items uniquely designed for the New York City commuter. According to an *InStyle* article in 2016, they planned to roll out the store to multiple locations in the coming years, but at this time the Canadian Lab stores have closed and they are exclusively operating in New York City at 50 Bond Street in Noho.[7]

Another example of this is Lululemon's men's-only store format, which was opened in New York and Toronto in 2017. This store included access to running group routes, events, a ping pong table, an on-site barber, and a cold brew bar. It was a short two-year run, and it closed at the end of 2018, even as Lululemon continued to invest in the growth of the menswear line.[8] "We continually test and learn at Lululemon – which is what we did with the men's stores,"

Erin Hankinson, a spokesperson for Lululemon, said, "After testing out the menswear stores, the retailer found that customers responded better to the company as a "dual-gender brand.""[9] This is worthy of note and applause, as much for their courage to try a unique experience model and see how it is received.

As announced at the National Retail Federation (NRF) Big Show in January of 2017, Lululemon continued to invest heavily in CRM data collection and machine learning to start profiling customer groups and gain insights into customer behaviors. A foundational step was encouraging educators in store to ask for e-mail addresses with every transaction. Previously anonymous customers were identified, customers were associated with their purchases, and customer online profile activity was used. Combined together, these became the anchor identifier used to evaluate the customer. This is the essence of many CRM strategies, capturing the full expanse of engagement activity both online and in-person. Doing so, often requires a value exchange, which can include offering content tailored to the customer or alerts of upcoming promotions or activities in the store. According to the EVP of Digital at the time, Miguel Almeida, this data was coupled with online customer feedback, comments on product pages, and real-time engagement via social channels including Facebook and Instagram. Lululemon even incorporated insights gathered in the call center. The goal, as articulated by Almeida, was to touch 1 billion people while providing a hyper-personalized experience based on insight gathered about the individual customer together with insight about others who shared a similar persona. As Almeida said, "Human relationship is at the core of who we are. It's never been only about physical products but always about creating a community hub as the core foundation."[10] He also led a redesign effort of the website, as it was not optimized for mobile and "not very seamless." These initial efforts had significant returns, driving 50% higher web visits and a 25% boost in attendance at local store events. This continuous and relentless focus on innovation and novel transformation of the experience to meet evolving needs of the customer drove consistent and significant returns.

NOVEL OMNICHANNEL ENGAGEMENT

As we've entered the post-digital transformation age, Lululemon is uniquely positioned to capture the modern generation's expectation of engaging experiences, novel capabilities, and truly seamless omnichannel engagement. Smartly, they haven't stood still, and they continue to introduce new and innovative experiences and solutions to engage customers. Entering the unprecedented era of the COVID pandemic in 2020, when customers were not patronizing stores, Lululemon bought Mirror, a wall-mounted, application-driven virtual workout solution that brought the yoga studio, cross-fit studio, and personal trainer into the home. While the in-home integrated fitness trend hasn't been a perfect growth story, and Mirror sales have reflected the challenges inherent to that product class in initial years postacquisition, it's still a smart strategy in the short term to bring the experience of the in-store fitness class, and the Ambassador engagement into the home. *Intelligence Automation* predicts in a 2022 article that 70% of people who used online fitness programs during the pandemic plan to stick with them long term.[11] As the younger generations – Millennials and Generation Z – continue to mature in life and in their careers, they will likely continue to be drawn to the idea of flexible engagement models, allowing them to patronize the store physically or virtually based on the schedule of the day.

Beyond that, Lululemon continued to evolve their digital strategy to provide a positive, community-centric experience in their stores. They had already invested in radio frequency identification (RFID) technology, which allowed them to temporarily convert stores to fulfillment centers. This helped them to easily accommodate the spike of online orders that occurred during the early days of the COVID pandemic lockdown.[12] They also implemented a number of new digital services, such as virtual waitlists that notified customers when they could enter the store – this was to address capacity restrictions in physical locations that were implemented during COVID – and mobile point-of-sales (POS) systems that allowed transactions such as returns, exchanges, or gift card purchases to be handled just outside the store. They expanded their buy online, pick up in store (BOPIS) and curbside pickup capabilities, and established the ability to set an appointment to shop before, during, and after the store's normal operating hours, again increasing the total capacity of the physical footprint while, equally, addressing the societal concerns that COVID instilled in the consumer population. Finally, and perhaps most cleverly of all, they rolled out virtual personal shopping guidance for customers that prefer to shop online but might require a little extra assistance.[13] All these capabilities were new, and while Lululemon's strategy was certainly reactive during the most turbulent time of the worldwide COVID lockdown, the success ties back to the novelty of the solutions and the recognition that such novelty creates.

Again, Lululemon's focus in this current post-digital transformation era isn't exclusively on selling more product. They continue to build the communities and connections on social media channels, including WeChat in China and a range of platforms in North America and Europe. During Lululemon's first week of store closures in March of 2020, at the very early stages of the pandemic, they had nearly 170,000 people join livestream classes on Instagram.[14]

What this reflects is a true transition of Lululemon's experience strategy to omnichannel, which was partially forced by the COVID pandemic but which will likely remain an expectation as the Millennial and Generation Z consumers continue to enter the marketplace and expand their buying power. In the words of the current CEO, Calvin McDonald, when speaking with CNBC's Jim Cramer in December of 2020, "Innovation, omni-guest experiences and market expansion make up Lululemon's growth strategy."[15]

As Lululemon looks forward to the future, they've taken the clever step of opening a global innovation center, bringing the innovation function together with in-house technology capabilities. As of this publication, their goal is to have 250 technologists employed by the center in 2022. According to current CTO, Julie Averill, as quoted in the *Times of India*, "All of our strategies are underpinned by technology – product innovation, omnichannel guest experiences or international market."[16] This

India-based team, according to the article, will focus on designing and developing a range of technology-enabled solutions that will improve the guest experience, both online and in store. The article also notes that other large retailers, including Target, Lowe's, Walmart, and Tesco, have centers in India that are helping digitize operations.[17]

This is the pinnacle of an innovation function, as this type of dedicated center brings together strategy and technology talent able to push forward several initiatives in rapid fashion, each of which can be tested in the market and measured for impact. I have personally observed a range of companies across the full spectrum of industries build similar functions in highly educated low-cost geographies. The key, which Lululemon articulates clearly in the *Times of India* article, is to ensure that all innovation efforts remain focused on improving the customer experience, providing new capabilities that capture attention and engagement while in parallel employing the other strategies laid out in the book, including reducing the time required to perform functions, leveraging data transparently and openly to improve personalization, and, ultimately, building the emotional connection that maintains loyalty to the brand.

BUILDING INNOVATION INTO YOUR BRAND STRATEGY

In all sincerity, this topic, more than any other, lends itself to several intriguing examples, each unfolding in recent years, that could be explored. Many of these are technology-centric, even though they serve within an industry other than tech. Uber is the perfect example; they took what was an absolutely terrible experience of hailing or securing a taxi, with the complete lack of transparency into availability, cost, and quality of vehicle, and created the perfect, novel experience on the smartphone. Apple continuously captured market attention through innovation in the product experience, engagement experience when using the product, and physical experience with the Apple stores. PayPal redefined financial transactions, which ultimately was somewhat eclipsed by the even simpler and somewhat social-oriented Venmo.

There are four key lessons that can be drawn from the Lululemon story and, generally, the impact that novel experiences have on brand activation, engagement, and loyalty. I encourage you to reflect on these companies' stories, and Lululemon's journey, to assess how these lessons can apply to your brand. Ultimately, there are four key lessons that should be gleaned from the high-growth, hyperloyal brand story I've described here.

First, don't introduce something new simply to create a splash. Ensure that the innovation aligns with your brand strategy and your experience strategy. Break down each experience in the customer funnel and ask the question of whether it addresses a need or gap that improves customer progression, while equally reflecting the tone and voice of the brand. In parallel, evaluate the idea through the lens of the entirety of the stage and the desired outcome of that stage. For example, if the novel idea extends the time required to complete the initial transaction, it's likely going to have a neutral to negative impact. Lululemon continuously grounded their innovation activities against the brand promise of high-quality clothing supporting an active and healthy lifecycle. Your brand should maintain similar alignment.

Second, remain focused and, when possible, keep the scope small. In most situations, speed to market is the top priority, and the window of novelty will be somewhat short. Novel is exactly that – it's new – but it is also fleeting, which is why continuous innovation is so critical. Building an AI-driven conversational interface that can be used to answer questions quickly with the level of interpretation previously reserved for human-to-human interactions might be exciting, but once successful in the market, it will likely be replicated within a year by your competition, requiring you to think about the next innovation. In today's post-digital transformation era, new design concepts, new navigations, and new functionality on your website or mobile application may draw interest and engagement for a short time, but likely you will be matched by your competition relatively quickly. Even physical rollouts, such as Lululemon's concept stores in Edmonton, Toronto, and New York, draw immediate buzz and traffic but lose momentum over time.

That doesn't diminish the value of the initiative, as short-term gain can be highly valuable. Every opportunity to drive engagement is accretive to the business and increases the opportunity to convert customers and ultimately drive customers toward loyalty. At the same time, the short-term impact cycle emphasizes the need for a continuous focus on innovation, and an equal focus on aligning that innovation with a customer need, a customer expectation, and the brand strategy. That is the key to success, and it's not a simple process. It requires investment, flexibility, and a willingness to accept failures on the path to success, as Lululemon has done.

A third lesson is to continuously measure impact, and don't invest beyond measurable gain. The colloquial phrase is "Don't throw good money after bad." This is complementary to the idea of short-term gain but extends further the idea that certain introductions will have a long tail for reasons other than being unique. In fact, certain novel experiences will become cornerstones of the experience. For Lululemon, that included, among other things, the Ambassador program and foundational elements of the omni-channel experience, including buy online, pick up in store. Other innovations ran for a short period, such as the men's-only concept store, and while the menswear line remains core to their strategy, the idea of a men's retail space had gains for several months but not years. To know what is sticking to the brand experience and what should be retired, data and analytics need to be applied against the initiative itself, so that impact can be measured, baselines can be set, and incremental gains and losses can be considered. Alongside this, fundamental experience studies such as a customer-experience survey should be completed, which would help identify where there are diminishing returns.

Finally, look to the future, but don't get too far ahead of your market or your brand. New experience concepts are appearing constantly, from the massive (the metaverse wave, outlined in Chapter 10, is a great example) to the trivial (redesigning the layout of the mobile application, for example). This full spectrum of innovation has the potential to appeal to your current and prospective customer bases. However, when evaluating ideas, it's important to understand who the target demographic is and how sophisticated they are. For example, if your target audience is primarily Generation X and Baby Boomers in the Midwest United States, rolling out a sophisticated cryptocurrency payment platform will likely not hit home. Building an entire shopping experience for women's apparel on a virtual reality (VR) platform will likely have a similar response, as VR remains primarily the domain of gamers and, predominantly, males. To the contrary, take an approach of incrementality, and find a need within the market that can be enhanced through innovation, technological connectivity, and compelling visualization. Align that approach with the current state of your market maturity, and then apply that approach to both digital physical and digital experiences. That combination was employed over and over again by Lululemon, and the return on investment was significant.

Coming back to Lululemon, the final question that needs to be asked is what, ultimately, was the impact to the business of this continuous innovation and novelty? To answer that, let's look at Lululemon's performance over the last five years. In 2017, Lululemon's revenue was $2.34 billion, whereas at the end of 2021 they reported $4.40 billion in revenue. The stock during the past five years is always moving, but it's up over 400% as of this writing. While part of this exponential growth is certainly attributed to product innovation, operational improvement, and effective merchandising, history has proven that a reasonable percentage of this can and should be attributed to their continuous cycle of innovation and association of innovation back to the customer journey and the brand that they maintained over their 24-year history.

CHAPTER 8

Humanizing the Experience

Throughout the previous chapters, the selected brand stories have clearly demonstrated that digital transformation has changed how every individual, regardless of relationship, demographic, and socioeconomic category now engages with brands. Consumers, business customers, employees, and partners worldwide now use a range of digital tools and technologies to communicate, inquire, and transact, regardless of whether they're in a remote rural area or the most crowded metropolis. This has reached a point, in this newly emerging post-digital transformation era, where digital has become invisible. Like air, we don't notice digital capabilities unless they're absent. It's a foundational expectation.

This was a topic I discussed in detail with other experts in preparation for this book. One person I had an opportunity to spend significant time with was Kaleeta McDade, who currently serves as the Global Executive Creative Director for Ogilvy Experience. Kaleeta is a brilliant mind who embraces the understanding that experience has become the foundation for defining the brand in the post-digital transformation era.

In our discussion, Kaleeta highlighted the rush to functionality that so many brands were forced to employ during the first full decade of the digital transformation era. Many brands followed a *Field of Dreams* strategy (a reference to the 1989 film released by Universal Studios), building functionality on multiple platforms and hoping that traffic would come. It's hard to criticize this approach, as it mirrors the novel innovation approach outlined in the previous chapter, but the speed of early innovation led to a mass commoditization. Every brand started to look like every other brand, every experience started to mirror every other experience, and function became the priority. The idea that humans, with needs, expectations, and most importantly emotions, were interacting with the experience became lost in the rush to production. Kaleeta continuously emphasized that this was an extraordinary miss, and many brands missed an opportunity because they didn't take the time to understand the fundamental human needs that would drive engagement with the experience.

UNDERSTANDING PEOPLE'S NEEDS

Kaleeta and I discussed several digital deployments that moved ahead of the societal need, missed critical market expectations, or failed to overcome initial challenges to the experience that turned off the user. One example is Kozmo.com, a digitally native company that promised "free one-hour delivery of videos, games, DVDs, music, magazines, books, food, basics, and more."[1] They even offered to deliver Starbucks coffee and had a partnership with Starbucks that allowed Kozmo customers to return videos to their local Starbucks store. It was a very clever and highly visionary model.

Launched in 1998 by Joseph Park and Yong Kang, the service was rolled out in several major cities in the United States, but, unfortunately, they took significant losses and never reached critical mass. Park and Kang blamed the market decline of 2000, often called the dot-com boom, and financiers point to the financial model of not charging delivery fees, but what emerges upon historical review of the business is that they were solving for a need that didn't yet exist.

In the late 1990s, the primary need was finding the product to buy, and for many of the core products they delivered, including videos, games, DVDs, music, magazines, and books, the browsing experience remained more important that the fulfillment process. Spending time in the CD aisles, or the video store, or even the grocery store, was inspirational and exciting. Discovery, or even the hunt itself, satisfied a critical human need, and the shopping experience was typically social. Since the online commerce industry hadn't yet reached a point of full discovery and real time information by 1998, the consumer was not prepared to remove that step in the journey. Engagement rates didn't generate the volume needed to offset the costs or propel continued investment.

To be clear, this wasn't the wrong idea, just the wrong time. Amazon clearly saw the potential for last mile, near immediate delivery, and they were one of the early investors in Kozmo.com.[2] They had introduced capability to the market before the market was ready for the service, and they were eliminating a key human need from a customer journey that trumped the convenience of at-home delivery. And while same-day grocery (and other product) delivery is now available from multiple brands, Kozmo.com missed the realization that they weren't meeting a specific human need. Now that the human need is addressed through the exponential expansion of Internet content, which allows consumers to browse, discover, and even sample products online, the opportunity for Kozmo.com models has expanded, and several companies, including but certainly not limited to Amazon, Instacart, Peapod, and DoorDash, all offer near-immediate last mile delivery. In fact Kozmo.com, which was purchased soon after closing operations, reopened in 2018 and now focuses on bulk deliveries of groceries with a small delivery fee.[3]

In our discussion, Kaleeta highlighted many other examples of companies that followed a similar path as a result of missing the human needs. Facebook eclipsed MySpace, even though MySpace had a three-year headstart in the marketplace. While they were almost identical in size in 2008, Facebook maintained a far closer understanding of what the market was looking for, while MySpace's, as

Cesar Cadenas articulates in a blog post on Screen Rant, "failure to focus on what its community wanted and the usability of the site saw users leave for other platforms."[4] This was driven partially or primarily by News Corp's acquisition of MySpace and a focus on monetization, which often was in direct conflict with the human need. Xerox, Napster, and LimeWire are other examples that come to mind.

While it's important to learn from companies that haven't succeeded, to ensure that your brand doesn't suffer from the same mistakes, it's more enlightening and energizing to highlight successful models that can be emulated and expanded to drive continued customer engagement and growth. There are many examples of brands that have recognized the unmet human need in the market, leveraging that understanding to capture outsized market share. Perhaps most notable in recent history is Apple, which as of the start of 2022 is the largest company when measured by market capitalization. In fact, at the time of this writing, their market share surpasses the second largest company by over $500 billion. That's a remarkable lead.

Apple reached this milestone by focusing on the human need – experience opportunity in every stage of growth and evolution. They were, arguably, the first company to mix fashion and technology, addressing the human need to appear distinctive and fashion forward, which caused people to desire the product even during periods when quality was relatively low and the price point was high. Apple also built emotional excitement, sense of want, thorough experiential panache, and unending confidence, drawing on the same societal desire to be unique and part of the latest buzzworthy trend. From Steve Jobs's famous on-stage product rollouts to the iconic Orwell-inspired 1984 Super Bowl advertisement that first introduced the Macintosh computer, Apple established an experience that did more than express nonconformity – it expressed superiority, exclusivity, and, generally, a coolness factor that the PC industry, and eventually the smartphone and smartwatch industry, have been unable to match. They maintained this with the iPhone launch in 2007, and people bought the product in droves even though the product didn't support corporate e-mail systems for almost a year, to be able to show their friends and colleagues that they were part of a select group. I was one of those people, and I often reflect on the superfluousness of the decision given that the first release was so expensive relative to my income, there were so few value-added applications available, the phone consistently dropped calls, and I still needed my BlackBerry to remain productive at work. I'm not knocking the iPhone, as I have consistently upgraded my phone and it's one of my more valued material possessions today, but back in 2007, it was more hype than reality.

This philosophy and approach, led by Steve Jobs and his relentless pursuit of design perfection, drove the success of most products. Apple's design and experience-led approach triggered multiple human emotional desires, including, as highlighted earlier, being part of the latest trends, of wanting to display fashion and design sense, and, generally, fear of missing out on cutting-edge functionality. This continues to be a human need that is addressed each time you visit the Apple Store today, one of the few retail formats that still draws people in, and often maintains a line of people waiting to attend. People want to be part of the sleek, modern experience populated with "geniuses," with products on display and available for exploration, and with associates walking around in black T-shirts and jeans. People want to be part of the environment and that experience.

Tesla is another example, proving their model with exponential market growth that has landed them fifth on the list of largest companies by market cap as of this writing. While Tesla vehicles continue to be relatively expensive, with their top end models costing more than most luxury brands but still taking about a year to reach the owner's driveway due to continuous manufacturing delays,[5] and their quality is an abysmal 30th out of 33 brands per JD Power,[6] Tesla topped the list in JD Power's 2020 APEAL study that measures owners' emotional attachment and level of excitement with their new vehicles.[7] Tesla was able to separate satisfaction from quality by following Apple's approach, which includes simplified configuration and ordering via the online portal, a retail showroom experience lacking the high-pressure sales tactics of the traditional dealership, and an unparalleled experience once sitting behind the wheel – the Tesla feels more like driving a computer simulator than a car. The cars themselves are the definition of modern car design, and the electric vehicle configuration adds status and addresses a common desire of people to help the environment.

Chewy.com recognizes the emotional attachment between people and their pets, and offers value-added services throughout the customer journey, including access to a veterinarian online, an AI-drive "ask anything" section to the site that helps owners with questions around pet behavior, condition, nutrition, and general wellness, and, perhaps most notably, Chewy.com sends a card and bouquet of flowers to customers who cancel their subscription due to loss of their companion. The emotional connection for many pet owners rivals or at least comes close to the connection with a child, and Chewy satisfies the human need to provide the best care and best quality of life for these cherished members of households.

Finally, beloved American QSR brand Chick-fil-A hires well-dressed, polite kids to stand outside and bust the line at the drive-through, conveying the energy and enthusiasm of youth while meeting the need of getting food into the car faster, all with a friendly "it was a pleasure to serve you" being conveyed by every employee. This meets the human need of being valued and appreciated as a customer, the foundation of great customer experience that has often been overlooked during the rush to digital transformation.

Any of these brands could serve as a detailed case study for the value of humanizing the experience across both digital and physical channels, but one that stands out due to their rapid growth and remarkable adoption rates in 2021 and 2022 is Robinhood.

EXPANDING AN EXCLUSIVE MARKET TO EVERYONE

As Kaleeta noted in our discussion, Robinhood is a brand that has leveraged a unique understanding of human needs and emotions to make a significant impact on markets in recent months. It's impossible to improve upon Kaleeta's natural eloquence, so to quote from our discussion, "Robinhood is revolutionizing financial services by reducing the pretentious divide. Challenging the financial service lexicon and breaking it down into easier, more relatable terms, Robinhood gave access to the masses while empowering a financial revolution that almost broke our brokerage system in 2021."

"The stock market is a fragile entity, based on intangible attribution of 'value' and worth, and these new participants are redefining both terms. This revolution will not be televised, but it will be socialized. Through new mechanisms of micro funding, social crowd funding, and a community willing to reverse the divide between the wealthiest minority and the hand-to-mouth majority, Robinhood's uniquely human approach to investing has been the preeminent leader in enabling financial evolution. With the shifts in spending to new asset classes, including cryptocurrency and NFTs, this decentralization of value definition will either create new streams of revenue or change the way we exist forever."

With that provocation, let's see what we can learn from Robinhood's story. According to their website, Robinhood's story begins almost a decade ago at Stanford, where Baiju Bhatt and Vladimir Tenev met as roommates and classmates. After graduation, they packed their bags for New York and built two finance companies, selling trading software to hedge funds. With their newfound experience in the world of finance, they realized that big Wall Street firms pay effectively nothing to trade stocks, while most Americans were charged a commission for every trade.

Bhatt and Tenev soon decided it was more important to build products that would provide everyone with access to the financial markets, not just the wealthy. Two years after heading to New York, they moved back to California and built Robinhood, a company that leverages technology to encourage everyone to participate in our financial system.[8] This origin story already expresses the human-centricity of the brand and a focus on meeting a societal need by providing the common person with access to investing tools and to markets that previously were viewed to be inaccessible.

When they launched, they actively communicated that traditional brokerages spend fractions of a penny to execute trades while charging fees of $5 to $10 per trade to their clients. Robinhood also noted that these traditional brokerages require account minimums of $500 to $5,000.[9] Meanwhile, Robinhood offered free trading and no account minimums.

This clearly met a unique need in the market, which eliminated the standard brokerage's significant barrier to entry, Tenev and Bhatt noted in a 2014 interview with *Forbes* magazine. They explained that of the 150,000 accounts that signed up before Robinhood's official launch, 75% of the clients were born in 1980 or later. They were capturing the attention and engagement of the highly valued Millennial Generation, leaving the established brokers to focus the older Generation X customers.[10]

HUMAN-FIRST ENGAGEMENT

Tenev and Bhatt knew that Millennials, their core demographic, didn't spend significant time on desktop and laptop computers, so they took a mobile-first approach, which was unique when they launched. The mobile application has evolved over the years, getting richer in functionality with each release, but it's built on a foundation of simplicity, transparency, and human-like connection. The phrases used during the sign-up process aren't formal or stiff but, instead, questions phrased similar to "What are you looking to do on Robinhood?" and "Want help with your first investment?" They communicate in a language at once familiar to the common person, and particularly to the Millennial and now Generation Z cohorts. The entirety of signup, which, in full disclosure, I went through in 2014, still maintains a feel very similar to the setup process for the iPhone: simple plain-English questions, drop-down answer boxes, and clear help icons if there's any questions along the way. Once the sign-up is completed, the Robinhood App reminds the person that they can start with as little as $1, removing a level of intimidation that is often created by large brokerages and their minimum balances.

As Robinhood evolved, they remained focused on building a mobile experience that was intuitive and easy. As founder Tenev shared with the Huffington Post in 2015, the initial focus was to build an application that kept the user engaged for 20–25 seconds, which he believed at the time was how long people would use a mobile application for. Tenev did admit that it was a difficult endeavor, but, ultimately, it was worthwhile, as Robinhood's design first philosophy resulted in the first financial product to win an Apple design award.[11]

This grounding in intuitive design and common language gave the app a human-like feel that assuaged the natural anxiety with putting scarce, hard-earned money into markets that many people barely understood. It certainly worked for Robinhood, who, according to their interview with Huffington Post in 2015, saw remarkably rapid growth immediately following launch. An early user – possibly the first to sign up – posted the application to Reddit, an American social news aggregation, web-content rating, and discussion website, and the number of new user sign-ups spiked quickly, to 30 visitors on the first evening of launch, and to 400 people the next day, which happened to be a Saturday. They gained over 100,000 sign-ups in their first 30 days. Ultimately, they ended up with a waitlist that was over 1 million strong.[12] This was all done without any advertising or proactive marketing; the brand was established through the experience and the viral nature of social networking. Robinhood quickly saw the value in this organic growth, and they rolled out a referral program, swapping three free stocks for every referral, while also giving the new client free stock as well.

Another technique that Robinhood employed was transparency, which invokes the natural human emotion of trust. Trust is one of the elements of foundational loyalty to the brand, which as we will see, Robinhood has maintained throughout their nine-year history. On their website and within this mobile app, they have a subsection entitled "How Robinhood Makes Money." They clearly articulate, in plain language most people can understand, how the trading process works, what the risks are, and what Robinhood protects the user from versus what is at risk.

Furthering the concept of humanization and addressing the inherent need of the individual, in 2017, Robinhood created a social media network. Interestingly, they launched it initially as a web platform, but, as articulated in a November 2017 Tearsheet article, most notable was the messaging for it: "To help to deliver the second part of [Robinhood's] mission to make stock trading accessible to everyday people; Help them make more informed decisions."[13] This approach mirrors the strategies employed at Amazon and Microsoft, two hypersuccessful companies that equally focused on the humanization of their experiences. In Leah Retta's *Dynamic Yield* e-book about recommendation-engine strategy and technology, they are quoted as saying "Discovery should be like talking with a friend who knows you, knows what you like, works with you at every step, and anticipates your needs," write Brent Smith and Greg Linden, two industry titans specializing in personalization and recommendations. From the onset, the end goal was to "harness the power of machines and data to humanize the digital experience for consumers."[14]

Bhatt embraced that sentiment when highlighting features designed to make trading more collaborative and social. For example, as Tearsheet explains in the same article, Robinhood shows, for any individual stock, how many other people own shares of that same company, the average price paid by other users for those shares, and the distribution of all the different prices people have paid for shares in the company in the past year. Bhatt outlined the value of this approach in very human terms, explaining that this approach made the data easier to understand, particularly for novice investors. By focusing on reference prices – how the current price compares to what other people have paid over time – Bhatt realized that people were starting not only to understand the data but also be able to make educated decisions based on what the individual stock was doing in the market.[15]

Cleverly, Robinhood adopted techniques employed by other successful human-first and digital-first brands, such as Amazon. They recognized that people who don't have significant time to investigate and research stocks, studying the advanced technical charts that day traders and professional financiers use in their craft, often look to friends and associates for stock-picking advice. They launched a recommendation tool similar to that employed by retail websites, showing stocks and other financial instruments that "people who own this stock have also invested in." It's not prompting the user to buy, but to investigate. As explained by Bhatt to Tearsheet, they took inspirations from online shopping sites, more specifically comparison shopping sites and music streaming applications. For example, the Robinhood app would show Morningstar's expert rating on the stock (e.g., 77% of analysts say buy), and they showed the number of Robinhood members who own the stock. The app maintains a For You section that suggests stocks to investigate based on buying and browsing data, and the app builds Playlists, which are collections of stocks matching a specific set of criteria such as virtual reality companies or the 100 most popular stocks of the year. Bhatt explained that, given the number of stocks that were available to be traded, it was always difficult to remember the one that you were looking for, so the application helped to make navigation and discovery easier through intuitive data-driven logic.[16]

There's a lot of information to unpack, but the essence of it is quite clear. Robinhood, from the beginning, recognized the importance of the familiar to the common investor. People are more comfortable when they're working in an environment that they recognize, interacting with capabilities that are familiar. That's true in the physical world, and it's true in digital experiences. So while other online trading platforms provided expert tools and detailed analytic interfaces that appeal to the sophisticated and confident trader, Robinhood recognizes that the uninitiated would be more at ease with an interface similar to commerce sites, social sites, and streaming sites. Clearly this tactic was working, as Robinhood crossed 3 million users, with $100 billion in transaction volume, near the end of 2017. That put them on par with e-Trade, which launched in 1996.

It's important to note that this is not disparaging of the other online trading platforms that were in operation at that time or in operation today. The tools and interfaces that e-Trade, TD Ameritrade,

Charles Schwab, and Scottrade have on the market are very good, highly functional, and extremely innovative. They are also highly successful in engaging and retaining the user profile that they targeted. They simply had subtle design differences, and a fundamental account model, that didn't appeal to specific demographics. Robinhood took advantage of this opportunity to engage these "everyman" cohorts, creating an experience that met a human need and building a business model that would address those needs.

RISKING CONTROVERSIES FOR GROWTH

Robinhood didn't stand still, continuing to roll out experience functionality that addressed the needs, expectations, and emotional triggers of their target client. They rolled out Robinhood Gold in 2017, which was a premium subscription that offered up to $50,000 in instant deposits, margin trading, and market analytics paralleling the more sophisticated online trading tools at the time. In 2018, they introduced cryptocurrency trading, a particularly hot topic among younger generations. Almost instantly after the announcement, the waitlist for this functionality grew to over 1.25 million. They later added support for Bitcoin Cash, Dogecoin, Ethereum Classic, and Litecoin, addressing the inherent distrust of financial service institution that existed among certain groups in the United States and worldwide.

Robinhood also maintains a simple and intuitive interface that emulates common online functions. For example, in the messaging section of the application, the interface looks very similar to social messaging or text messaging applications that are often used; it could be WhatsApp, iMessage, or GroupMe. Similar to the latter, it even prompts the user with common inquiries that can be selected with a touch of the screen. For example, when a trade is pending, and the message app shows the detail of the order, three prompted responses are, "Can I see more details?" (with a glasses emoji), "Why hasn't this order been filled yet?" (with a questioning/hand on chin emoji), and "Actually, I'd like to cancel this order" (with a red circle with a diagonal line emoji, often referred to as the No Symbol). It's not free-form, as it's not a true chat function, but it does address common inquiries quite effectively. Further, the application prompts the individual to customize their profile, asking questions about preferred investment vehicles, preferred industries, and other elements that customize the articles and the recommendations presented. The app continues to recognize the individuality of each investor and builds on that personal connection the way a friend would, keeping everything inviting, friendly, and most of all, in plain English, with almost gamelike graphical automation that is again familiar and comfortable for their primarily digitally native user base.

As observed with other brands, Robinhood's growth story isn't without controversy. Recognizing the Young Millennial and Generation Z trend towards alternative fintech models, they filed for a banking license and in December of 2018, they introduced checking and savings accounts, promising an exceptionally high interest rate for the time of 3%; at the time of the announcement the highest rate on a savings account from a licensed bank was 2.36%. They then claimed that these accounts would be Securities Investor Protection Corporation (SIPC) insured, which the SIPC denied.[17] This led Robinhood to take the offer off their website, canceling the waitlist. Nine months later, they introduced a Federal Deposit Insurance Corporation (FDIC)-insured cash management product, with a 2.05% interest rate that was still higher than average rates offered by traditional banks at the time. They had a significant outage in March of 2020, causing the site to go down three times during one of the most active and volatile periods – mostly a decline – in stock market history, preventing their customers from responding or reacting to the temporary dive. Remarkably, these events did little to slow the momentum of subscriber growth, which is a testament to the humanization of the Robinhood experience and the loyalty that that this human-experience helps generate.

Their total assets under management, the typical size measurement for a brokerage, are much smaller than the major firms, but given that their model is to capture the attention and engagement of the smaller investor, this is not surprising. Their current subscriber base numbers, quite notably, over 22 million as of the third quarter of 2021, which makes them a force in the marketplace. A good portion of this success can be attributed to their continuous focus on humanization of their experience and their ability to connect with the unsophisticated and novice investor, skewing to the younger generation that has grown up in a digital world and expects this type of experience from the sign-up through servicing.

It's easy to reflect on Robinhood's story and dismiss it as an example of a digital-first brand that eclipsed the rest of the market because they weren't burdened by the infrastructure or inherent costs that are part of the traditional brand. However, in reality, that's not the case. Any existing enterprise could have extended their offering to replicate what Robinhood developed, and they would have been aided by having an existing infrastructure that was far more robust than the lean start-up that they maintained in their early days. Digital-first brands certainly have flexibility, but that flexibility comes with a cost, including a lack of operating capital, limited resources, and nonexistent processes. I can speak from personal experience when I say that operating a startup in its early days can be, at times, chaotic, but it's the culture of flexibility that gives these entities an advantage.

The other argument that could be made is that Robinhood captured their market share through an exceptional and unprofitable offering. Robinhood certainly did capture initial market share in 2014 with its offer of zero cost trading, but the large brokerages rapidly caught up and offered that a few years later. Yes, Robinhood did have an exceptional offer, but their offer was driven from the recognition that charging per trade was a barrier to entry for many casual traders that wasn't necessary for economic viability.

Robinhood's continued growth was in large part driven by their continuous attention to humanizing the experience, and their unwavering focus on meeting their clients where they were, providing the tools, the information, and the transparency necessary to encourage engagement, commitment, and, ultimately, loyalty.

HUMANIZING EFFECTIVELY

So, what can be learned from the Robinhood story? There are five lessons that can be leveraged as you work to develop your human need–experience strategy.

As discussed in detail throughout this chapter, first and foremost it's critical to develop an understanding of your brand's target population and addressable market. This must include both explicit and implicit needs, so it goes beyond the market survey and net promoter score (NPS) analysis, requiring deep observation of demographic and socio-economic trends through a lens of psychology and behavioral science. Once you've developed that understanding of your brand's addressable market, you can separate members of this market into segments, with associated personas, that can be evaluated against the brand and product strategy. This allows your brand to focus its experience design efforts, and more specifically, its experience humanization efforts, against these personas and their specific emotional triggers. Robinhood, for example, recognized that it wasn't going to convince the high-net-worth investor, or even the affluent investor, to shift their assets over to their fledgling platform. The opportunity to build trust and confidence without the backing of an established financial services entity was too high a hill to climb. Equally, they recognized that many novice investors were being left out of the markets due to fear of the unknown and the minimum balance and cost-per-trade structures. Therefore, they structured their product offering to address the financial barriers and then designed their interface to specifically target, attract, inspire, and retain the novice investor who was likely younger, digitally savvy, and somewhat wary of "traditional" financial institutions.

Second, it's important to map the entirety of the customer experience, recognizing that in this post-digital transformation era, the journey may not be linear. Given the richness of search engine results, and the range of search platforms, including Google, YouTube, Facebook, Amazon Echo, and many others, together with industry-specific search platforms such as Yelp!, Healthgrades, OpenTable, and others, customers will engage with the brand through a range of paths, equipped with information and a perspective that is already establishing their perception of your brand. While it's impossible to anticipate every entry point, it's critical that you recognize the in-and-out nature of customer engagement today, and the recognition that customers will not follow a fixed path. By humanizing your experience, you can guide the visitor to the right point in the journey based on where they are, without frustrating them and leading them to abandon you. Take advantage of CRM data and encourage the customer to identify themselves, which will allow you to pick up the interaction with the customer where you believe it to have been left off. However, for those customers that prefer anonymity, offer a path to a logical point in your experience, using plain English and clear instructions. Think of it as the digital version of your brand greeter, whose role is to answer any questions and, ultimately, guide visitors to where they want to go. Robinhood is quite adept at this, providing deep link access (access to specific functional pages that are accessed from search engines and other sources) that allows expert users to perform a function or complete an inquiry, but equally offers navigation to the start of the journey for those who landed in the spot erroneously or blindly. An example of humanization would be to present a simple question to the visitor who's directly landed on a deep link page with the phrase, "Not sure how you got here? I can help." This would then either link to the home page, or even better, ask a simple question of "What are you looking to do?" Again, it feels more interactive and intelligent than just showing a basic menu across the top or left side. The same approach applies to all channels; For example, with your Alexa skill, if you're going to enable Alexa to perform basic tasks, make sure that Alexa understands plain English. Don't force your customer to relive the horrific days of interactive voice response (IVR) jail – configure your voice interface to interpret meaning in multiple ways. It'll have a massive impact on conversions.

Third, as highlighted in the Robinhood example but also exemplified in many of the brands that embrace this philosophy, use common design patterns and interaction models that are standard on digital platforms. Robinhood employs a messaging interface that feels identical to WhatsApp and iMessage, for example. Robinhood's application also adheres to Apple's Human Interface Guideline (HIG) design standards, including MacOS, iOS, watchOS, and tvOS, which make the application feel more intuitive and natural. Proceed with caution, however, as you don't want to fall into the commoditization trap that Kaleeta highlighted early in this chapter. It's critical to retain a distinct and unique identity and personalization for the experience to effectively define your brand position, but the tone and style can be unique even with the fundamental methods of interaction are commonplace.

Fourth, don't forget about the value of your data. Human beings naturally gather information, both consciously and unconsciously, during in-person interactions. Everything from what is discussed and communicated to facial expressions and inflections in speech. Digital experiences don't yet have that capability, although there are some emerging technologies that are attempting to bring that to market. For now, data needs to replace human intuition, and analytics, enhanced by artificial intelligence, can help to profile the customer, anticipate the need, and tailor the interaction to make it even more natural. Robinhood is quite effective at this, prompting up front the ability for the client to create a profile and specify areas of interest and areas of expertise. Robinhood starts tailoring the application experience right at that initial moment, and then continues to tailor the experience with each subsequent interaction. This emulates what a great salesperson or customer service representative naturally does as they build a relationship with the prospect or customer.

To that end, don't forget the value of data-driven insights for your in-person interactions as well, as it will allow your team to more effectively serve the needs of the customer. In today's post-digital transformation era, it's assumed that interactions cross the digital and the physical seamlessly, and your data store is the intersection point for experiences.

Finally, don't lose sight of the overall brand strategy and how it aligns with experience strategy over time. There are many examples of brands that did a complete overhaul of their digital experience to reflect modern functionality or design standards, but in doing so, lost the style, tone, and visualization that defined the brand. Not only is it jarring to the customer when they visit and discover a new experience, but it can be frustrating if the voice and style of the experience completely shifts, just as it would be if the same customer walked into an office, branch, or store to discover the employee's look, tone, and style completely shifted. It's critical to continue to evolve with the market and continue to innovate and expand the information and capabilities accessible across every channel, but when doing so it's equally critical to remain grounded in the overall strategy and the current understanding of the target market's expectations and needs. Robinhood embraced this understanding throughout its short history, maintaining its focus on its target market, and maintaining its unique tone and style throughout many transformations. This created an experience strategy tailored to its target market and defined market persona, and it never wavered from that strategy as it continued its growth trajectory.

CHAPTER 9

Connecting Your Customer with Your Cause

One of the most significant shifts in modern brand management has been the adoption and emphasis of corporate social responsibility. As Tim Stobierski defines it in a Harvard Business School post, "Corporate social responsibility (CSR) refers to the concept that a business is not only responsible for creating value for shareholders, but should also seek to benefit the broader community within which it exists."[1] I couldn't have said it better.

Brands today recognize that the modern consumer demands to know what the company stands for and how they articulate those values. Over the last decade, that has expanded to become an expectation that the brand is contributing to the betterment of society in some way, and customers look for transparency in action. This is particularly the case with the younger generations – namely, Millennials and Generation Z – who are rapidly emerging as the spending force in the marketplace across B2C and B2B industries. This book is certainly not a forum for wading into the various pools of societal and geopolitical issues, so I won't name any specific causes or initiatives in particular, but suffice to say that brands have been embracing a range of causes, some timeless and some quite specific to the moment, over the past few years.

EMBRACING CORPORATE SOCIAL RESPONSIBILITY

That said, the idea of corporate social responsibility and, more broadly, institutional social responsibility, is not new. The *International Journal of Corporate Social Responsibility* outlines the rich history behind CSR, tracing its roots back to ancient Roman societies and through the various historical eras including the Middle Ages, Victorian period, and, more recently, the Industrial Revolution into the first half of the twentieth century. Academic, municipal, and religious institutions embraced various social causes within specific societies, often focusing on the poor, the disabled, and the orphaned. As the concept of the corporation emerged, early brands embraced the idea of CSR, including Macy's, which contributed to an orphan asylum as early as 1875, and Pullman Palace Car Company, which in 1893 created a model industrial community to improve the quality of life for their employees.

The concept of CSR truly began to gain traction in the 1970s, during a decade when the world saw organized protests against what portions of society considered to be injustices. This time, of course, was an evolution from the turbulent 1960s, where rebellion against authority became a defining foundation of the younger generation. The United States divided over many topics, most notably Vietnam but across several other civil and societal topics as well. The dynamics of politics, music, and popular culture changed, as 1967 brought the summer of love in San Francisco, and 1969 brought the Woodstock festival. This wasn't the entirety of the United States population, and certainly wasn't the entirety of the world population, but a reasonable percentage of this generation started to redefine what they viewed to be important and how they expressed their values. The first Earth Day was celebrated in the United States in 1970, with a significant focus on corporate pollution, such as oil spills, toxic dumps, and fossil fuel emissions. These efforts led to the creation of several regulatory bodies in the United States, including the Environmental Protection Agency (EPA), and other regulatory bodies worldwide. This, in turn, led to new requirements and restrictions being placed on corporations that forced changes to be made. Other similar protests, and similar regulatory rules, were implemented worldwide. Many corporations tried to challenge these regulations and changes, arguing that the increase in costs and the associated complexity of converting their processes for manufacturing and distribution would harm the economy, but many brands rapidly recognized that this narrative was alienating a large and important segment of their addressable market. Given that they were forced to make the changes to meet the regulatory requirements, savvy companies recognized that there was brand value in highlighting these changes, using words such as "clean" and "eco-friendly" to promote their social responsibility and frame this as part of their brand image.[2] While I have no particular insight or documentation to draw from, other than editorial posts, it's not a stretch to assume that many brands embraced of these social causes publicly in their brand messaging but secretly fought them in the boardroom and executive offices of the corporations, where the focus remained squarely on profits and on creating value for shareholders.

This changed in the late 1970s when a select number of brands had emerged that took a different response to corporate social responsibility. These companies did not simply express their support for societal issues; they embraced them at their core. They were built upon the foundation of a social cause, and the ethos penetrated all aspects of their brand, products, and operations.

One example is The Body Shop, which from its founding in the U.K. in 1975 proudly declared that they do not test cosmetic products on animals, declaring it unethical. Their origin story states with pride that "[The Body Shop] began . . . with a belief in something revolutionary: that business could be a force for good. We've never been your average cosmetics company, with over 40 years of campaigning, change-making and smashing beauty industry standards – and we're still going strong."[3] The Body Shop went on to champion many animal protection causes worldwide, working with the People for the Ethical Treatment of Animals (PETA), the Royal Society of the Protection of Cruelty to Animals (RSPCA), and other worldwide organizations to promote a "more humane lifestyle" and champion the cause of not testing cosmetics on animals as a platform against animal cruelty more broadly.[4] They truly led from the front in terms of building a company, and a brand, around a cause, and they continue to support this cause 50 years later.

Another example is Ben & Jerry's, the ice cream maker founded in Vermont in 1978. From the beginning, Ben & Jerry's has maintained the mantra that "business has a responsibility to the community and the environment."[5] The company built its brand on a clear set of core values and has lived them in every aspect of product development, operations, and employee development. Externally, it began donating 7.5% of their pretax earnings to social causes in 1985, and they supported multiple causes such as Greenpeace and the Vietnam Veterans of America. They have proudly invested in community-based products, including the Vermont Dairy Farm Sustainability Project, and they promote the use of Fair Trade products across their manufacturing process. As with The Body Shop, Ben & Jerry's parent company, Unilever, continues to embrace the brand's commitment to CSR and continues their practice today.[6]

There are many other examples of brands that were built on a foundation of business ethics and standards throughout the decades leading up to and throughout the age of digital transformation. These companies were often built on the vision and passions of their founders who saw an opportunity to support a societal cause and built their business around that opportunity. Salesforce.com's founder, Marc Benihoff, is known for his focus on philanthropy and charitable giving, and Salesforce Foundation was created to support a range of nonprofit organizations and educational institutions. Toms Shoes pioneered what it called the One for One model, giving away one pair of shoes to the underprivileged for every pair it sells.[7] The company retired this practice in 2019, but not before it donated over

95 million shoes. Now, according to the prominent "Impact" section of their website, they invest 33% of their profits in grassroots efforts, organizations creating change at the local level, and groups driving progress from the ground up.[8] The Taco Bell Foundation has contributed more than $114 millions in grants and scholarships to individuals looking to invest in their careers.

It's interesting to note that each of these brands has championed its causes, at times, to the detriment of their financial performance. There are blogs and financial publication articles readily available that highlight the impact that these initiatives have on the bottom line of the company, but given the emphasis that these companies continue to apply against their CSR vision, it's clear that they don't exclusively exist for performance. This level of commitment to the cause is truly impressive to see, and I applaud them for that.

SHIFTING FROM BRAND IDENTITY TO SOCIAL CAUSE

More recently, however, there's been a fundamental shift in the marketplace, not dissimilar to the shift that was observed in the early 1970s. Just as the early 1970s saw a focus, particularly but not exclusively among the younger, emerging generations, on societal issues and the impact that corporations were having on societal issues, today's consumers – indexing toward Millennials and Generation Z but again crossing every demographic – the past five years have seen a dramatic increase in focus on the overall ethos and specific social responsibility that a brand and the corporation express and embrace.

There is a distinct difference between the early 1970s and the early 2020s, and it's important to understand this distinction when discussing its impact on brand experience strategy. The early 1970s, carrying over from the 1960s, is often described as a time of distrust. It was a time of us versus them, of David versus Goliath. Individuals saw corporations and brands as evil. Again, not every consumer felt this way – far from it – but a percentage of the population that was large enough to warrant action did. The 2020s could be better described as a time of alignment. Consumers today are looking to engage with brands, across industries and across geographies, that express a vision and purpose that is meaningful to them. In many ways, the customer relationship has shifted away from an emotional connection to the brand itself and toward an emotional connection with the brand's social cause. Again, this isn't the case with every consumer, but it definitely is a significant enough percentage of the Millennial and Generation Z population to warrant action.

This shift has been dramatic and noticeable. According to a 2019 Aflac study, 77% of consumers are motivated to purchase from companies committed to making the world better.[9] A recent Deloitte survey indicated that 70% of Millennials acknowledged that a company's commitment to social responsibility influenced their choice to work there.[10] *Forbes* reinforced in a 2019 article that "Today's consumers are belief-driven. This means that, unlike traditional consumers, who may have prioritized price or convenience, they want to see brands that improve the world along with making a profit. The 2018 Edelman Earned Brand[11] study reports that this is a worldwide phenomenon. Furthermore, people are increasingly looking to brands, rather than to governments, to solve problems."[12]

The brands highlighted throughout this book are leading from the front in embracing social causes. For example, the *Forbes* article pointed out that Starbucks took a stand in supporting gay marriage and also partnered with universities to help young adults afford college.[13]

Amazon has funded a range of high-impact programs: environmental sustainability programs designed to achieve net zero carbon emissions and waste across packaging, shipping, and operations; supply chain transparency that ensures wage equity, worker safety, gender equality, and environmental sustainability; employee improvement programs that promote a diverse and equality-driven workplace given access to scholarships and training; and community outreach programs that address housing and food insecurity, education support, and, more recently, COVID-19 relief. As one of the most well-capitalized corporations in the world, Amazon recognizes the importance of paying forward and giving back to the local community and the worldwide society.[14]

Nike has supported several significant social causes including quite notably Colin Kaepernick's decision in 2016 not to stand for the National Anthem at NFL football games and running a 2018 campaign entitled "Believe in something. Even if it means sacrificing everything."[15]

Lululemon, like many modern brands, has focused on sustainability and environmental impact, highlighting prominently on their website that "We are deeply connected to ourselves, each other and our plant; each part elevating one another. We aim to create healthier environments by inspiring positive change through mindful choices, innovation and collaboration." The page details a supply chain strategy that "addresses greenhouse gas emissions across their operations" that could negatively impact global communities, oceans, forests, and ecosystems, and a packaging and waste strategy that is "taking steps to eliminate, reduce, reuse, or recycle where possible."[16] Adidas and Panera Bread have supported similar, equally inspirational causes across the world.

These brands are truly leading from the front, embracing and demonstrating their commitment to societal and environmental improvement every day. While it's plausible to believe that, like the 1970s, there are brands that are expressing a commitment to corporate social responsibility publicly while working to avoid the actual investment privately, it's far more difficult to maintain that strategy today in the world of always-on social media. Employees don't hesitate to communicate publicly and transparently about their employer, and if their employer does not demonstrate their commitment to their expressed cause, they will be called out quickly by the people whose role it is to embrace the vision in their daily work.

However, as we enter the post-digital transformation era, the consumer's expectations are continuing to evolve. As Kaleeta McDade, Global Executive Creative Director for Ogilvy Experience, explained to me, "In today's world, you have to move from category to culture, and you have to immerse the customer in the culture." Emotional connection to the brand is enhanced by this cultural connection, and now, the post-digital transformation consumer doesn't simply look to connect with brands that support their values and cultures. They expect to connect with brands that offer opportunities for the consumers themselves to impact the social causes that matter to them. As with other elements of brand connection, corporate social responsibility has shifted from exclusively a brand-communication initiative to a brand-experience initiative.

AUTHENTIC AND PROACTIVE LEADERSHIP

All the brands highlighted thus far in this book lead from the front in embracing the need to engage the individual – prospects, customers, and employees – directly in their causes. However, one brand stands above the rest in embracing this opportunity: Patagonia.

Patagonia's origin story is a bit different from what many people would expect. The founding team of Yvon Chouinard and Tom Frost, two mountain climbing enthusiasts, combined together in 1965 to form Chouinard Equipment, working together to create a better set of climbing tools for mountaineering worldwide. They're credited with the design and development of the Hexcentric climbing hexes that are still used in climbing today. They rapidly grew to be the largest climbing hardware company in the United States by 1970, due to both their innovations and to their celebrity within the industry.[17]

At this earliest stage, Yvon and Tom demonstrated their commitment to the environment. In 1970, in their own words, "Chouinard Equipment . . . had become an environment villain because its gear was damaging the rock. The same fragile cracks had to endure repeated hammerings of pitons during both placement and removal, and the disfiguring was severe."[18] This led Chouinard Equipment to minimize their piton business, leading to 70% turnover, but two years later they introduced aluminum chocks that are a big improvement. This pivot paid off, and aluminum chock demand exceeded

Chouinard's production capacity by 1972.[19] Consider that Chouinard made this pivot not due to governmental regulation but instead pro-actively, confirming that their core focus and ethos of the company was to protect the environment within which their products were used. That same year, Patagonia began producing clothing products that have become the foundation of their brand. The now ubiqui-tous Patagonia logo was introduced in 1975, featuring a silhouette of Mount Fitz Roy in the Patagonia region between Argentina and Chile, and Patagonia started investing in environmental causes including the clean-up of the Ventura River. This was the first of many preservation and clean-up efforts that Patagonia ultimately sponsored and invested in.

However, Patagonia's focus on social causes didn't only extend into environment. Patagonia was one of the first companies to pro-vide on-site childcare for employees, in 1983, and they opened an on-site cafeteria serving organic food to employees in 1984. They continued to lead from the front both externally and internally for the next three decades. Their journey wasn't without its challenges – Patagonia was on the verge of bankruptcy in 1991 during the reces-sion that started that decade – but overall, they've been able to realize a growth trajectory, build a global brand that's distinctive and valued in the market, and drive significant and measurable impact across a number of causes important to the company, its founders, and its employees.

ENGAGING AND INSPIRING THE COMMUNITY

That brings us to the current post-digital transformation era and this pivot to experience as the entry point for many prospective customers to the brand. Patagonia recognized several years ago, far before most organizations, that positive impact to the planet and positive impact to its employees requires people to get involved. Further, Patago-nia knew that its social responsibility pledge was an opportunity to engage its communities and customers, and the company extended

its investments to create experiences that the consumer could participate in directly. This is reflected on its website, where Patagonia ded-
icates half of its navigational real estate to experiences aligned with its
corporate mission of supporting the environment and engaging with
nature: Activism and Stories.

The Activism section of Patagonia's online experience offers
opportunities to gift funds to causes in a loved one's name, creating
a gift that extends far beyond the value of the donation. They offer
environmental action events, they offer petitions, and they offer
a listing of volunteering opportunities. All this is exposed as a Yelp!
like experience, where you can enter your location and see a list of
environmental groups you can join, events you can participate in, to
give back, to make an impact, or simply to connect with like-minded
people. There's very little Patagonia branding on this section of the
page, but the pathway to the page is clear, and Patagonia clearly gains
a halo effect benefit that extends beyond the cause itself. This is an
innovation approach to driving investment in their sponsored causes,
and, by providing more than simply a mechanism for cash donation
or a demonstration of commitment, they are leveraging the experience to build unparalleled loyalty within their customer base.

The Stories section of the site is filled with inspirational experiences.
While not directly tied to the social cause, it's filled with audio, video,
and text-based stories of people engaging with the environment. As the
page currently describes at the time of this publication, "Share experiences and powerful stories with your favorite people. It can strengthen
your bond and inspire them to take action. Here are a few stories we feel
are worth sharing."[20] One currently featured story, "Life Lived Wild,"
is listed as a five-minute read and describes the life of Rick Ridge-
way, an individual who *Rolling Stone* called the real Indiana Jones.[21]
It's a fascinating story, complete with high-resolution photography of
mountaineers and hikers enjoying jaw-dropping backdrop landscapes,
which certainly inspire the outdoor enthusiast to get outdoors. It's not
until the end of the story that you discover, in the author biography,
that Rick spent 15 years, beginning in 2005, overseeing environmental
affairs at Patagonia. Another story on the site at the time of this writing,

"Was it Worth It?" was penned by Doug Peacock, an American naturalist, outdoorsman, and bestselling author who cofounded several conservation organizations.[22] The stories available on this site are interesting, engaging, easy to consume, and inspiring.

In addition to the print stories, there are several films of varying lengths – from about 10 minutes to 40 minutes – and they are equally engaging. I spent ten minutes watching a video called "Run to Be Visible," in which the narrator and primary character, Lydia, talks about running and the culture of her community near Tucson, populated with indigenous people with a strong connection to the land.[23] She talks about the impact of progress and mining on the land and what that means to her and her community. It was engaging, informative, and inspiring. The films compel the visitor to stay on the site and explore other videos. It adds value far beyond the traditional brand value, and naturally builds an emotional connection between the visitor, the consumer, and the Patagonia brand, which, at the same time, demonstrates Patagonia's commitment to social responsibility.

It's important to note that Patagonia remains a brand in the business of apparel sales, even though it's easy to forget that when you are engaged with its experience, both online and in store. Their social cause messaging is strong enough that the products and merchandising become almost secondary, but the effect is significant. It connects a consumer, passionate about the same cause, to the brand, and inspires the consumer to become a customer, to both contribute to the environment – Patagonia donates 1% of revenue to the social cause – and, because the digital experience is exactly that, to have an experience that provides value far beyond the product shopping and commerce functionality.

COMMITTING TO THE CAUSE

Patagonia is an exceptional example of a brand driving a larger cause, and in and of itself it represents a cautionary tale. In today's post-digital transformation era, it is important for your brand to define and articulate what your brand stands for in the world and how the brand is making a positive impact in the world in some way, shape, or form, but at the same time, this needs to be a cause that the company will embrace. Unlike the companies from the last century that were forced to adopt changes due to regulatory restrictions, if your company only articulates the narrative and doesn't back that narrative up with clear action, the power of social media and other real-time communication channels will expose the brand. If you're going to commit to a CSR strategy, either externally in the world or internally with your employees, be certain that your entire organization is truly committed to the impact that you are expressing. If the commitment is not there, for whatever reason, it's better not to engage at all, as the negative effect can be devastating to the brand.

If the brand is prepared to commit to the cause, it's not necessary to invest at the level of Patagonia, which was built on the foundation of environmental protection. There is still significant opportunity to create distinction for the brand through the experience itself, and it's perfectly acceptable to both support a cause that drives a positive outcome and leverage the cause to also create deeper brand loyalty, as long as the loyalty is not developed at the cost of the cause. While I applaud Patagonia's unwavering focus and commitment, and the market has rewarded that commitment in the form of loyalty and brand value, it's possible to gain value from smaller, incremental steps. That's the key lesson that can be gleaned from the Patagonia story.

For example, at the lowest level of time investment, the consumer may decide to contribute some amount of money to the cause, which is a common model that brands follow through foundations and other methods. To extend this experience and create a connection with the individual, consider the approach that Patagonia embraces and, rather than just offer a mechanism for collecting donations, provide an opportunity for the contributor to see the impact of their donation. One method would be through a digital visualization tool, tracking the specific donation to a specific outcome. Even something as simple as a thermometer graphic showing how all the contributions are helping achieve a monetary goal, and then showing the result of the investment, such as a video of the new school that the donation funded, would draw the person into the experience of philanthropy and build a greater emotional connection both with the philanthropic cause and with the brand.

For slightly more time investment, perhaps offer an opportunity for the consumer to participate directly in the cause. Sponsor an event that impacts your cause and drives a positive outcome, and then invite a segment of the population – it could be an invite-only event for customers or a general call to the community – to participate. It's a chance to invest marketing funds into an activity that drives greater good while creating a deeper emotional connection with the customer.

Also, remember that experience doesn't need to be in the form of direct philanthropic activity or donation. Education is valuable to those individuals aligned with your purpose, and providing an opportunity to learn more, perhaps through interactive experiences either online or in a physical location, consumers can gain a better understanding of what's driving the cause. Articles and videos are wonderful mechanisms of engagement, and, when coupled with interactive experiences, will bring customers and prospective customers back to the brand. It becomes a win-win for the brand and for the cause and aligns you with the target market in a positive and highly accretive way.

The key is to be committed and focused on the positive outcome, but, equally, remember that the business is still in existence to provide a product or a service. Aligning the two through experience is an exciting and inspiring approach to growth, customer loyalty, and employee loyalty.

CHAPTER 10

Looking to the Future

Chapters 4 through 9 cover six key strategies that brands can employ to capture customer attention, drive customer commitment, and, ultimately, foster customer loyalty through experience strategies. In this new post-digital transformation era, when it's impossible to predict when and how the customer will engage with your brand, adopting one or all of these strategies will likely have a positive effect on your marketing and sales key performance indicators (KPIs) across the customer funnel, engaging more customers in an evaluative dialogue, encouraging more customers to transact and commit, and, once converted, inspire those customers to both return to the brand and advocate for the brand in public forums.

However, when I'm working with clients to define their experience strategy and shape their approach to this rapidly changing era, inevitably the conversation steers to the question of "These strategies are great, but the world keeps evolving. What do I need to be preparing for next that I can start to invest in today?" It's a great question, and one that I encourage every brand to explore. While there are plenty of initiatives that your teams can and should invest in today, it's important to keep an eye on the future and consider what opportunities are emerging to differentiate the experience, create novelty, demonstrate innovation, and, overall, reinforce your brand strategy.

Predicting the future, in all sincerity, is an exercise in educated guessing. As satirist P. J. O'Rourke famously quipped, "Predicting innovation is something of a self-canceling exercise: the most probable innovations are probably the least innovative."[1] In other words, if you already see that a future innovation is going to be adopted, you're likely late to the game. Others have already plowed that ground, proven it out, and captured the early imagination and attention of the marketplace.

INNOVATION WITH A LARGE I

As outlined in Chapter 7, Finding a Novel Approach to Solving a Market Need, innovation is critical and needs to be an area of continuous focus but, equally, an area of wise investment. Great experience ideas can be gleaned from global shows, including the Consumer Electronics Show held in Las Vegas every January and the Mobile World Congress held in Barcelona every February, as well as from articles in forward-thinking publications, observations in the market, and creative ideation among the team. That said, the term *innovation* itself can easily get confusing. The novel approaches outlined in Chapter 7 are actually incremental innovation, or "innovation with a small i"; it's strategic and highly impactful, but it's incremental.

This chapter is focused on transformative innovation, or "Innovation with a large I." These include ideas that bring the brand experience into a new realm, with a completely new channel paradigm, a rethinking of data leverage, and a fresh view on how to engage and build loyalty with the customer.

Interestingly, when looking for inspiration of this level, the science-fiction genre is a good source. The iconic author Isaac Asimov is often credited with predicting 10 significant advancements that have all been introduced today. Movies like *Minority Report* and *Terminator* reflected the potential of gesture-based interfaces, advanced wearable technology, and AI-driven interactions. Google even went back to the original *Star Trek* sci-fi series for inspiration, with Amit Singhal, Google vice president and senior search engineer, telling London's *Daily Mail* in 2012 that ". . . the company has been inspired by sci-fi series *Star Trek* to develop the 'ubiquitous computing' concept, where gadgets woven into users' daily lives seamlessly respond to questions."[2] Ultimately, this led to inspired solutions such as the AI-enabled Google Nest Speaker, Google Smart TV, and Google Glass. Singhal confirmed in the *Daily Mail* interview that Google Glass was partially inspired by *Star Trek*'s Lieutenant Geordi La Forge, who wore a wearable to offset his character's blindness.

That said, there are a few enterprises in the unique position of being able to truly experiment at scale. Look to the FAANG (Facebook, Amazon, Apple, Netflix, and Google) companies: Alphabet, the parent company of Google, is one such company, as demonstrated earlier. Apple is another, Amazon is a third, and Meta, the parent company of Facebook, is a fourth. These companies have built previously unimaginable market capitalizations and cash reserves that they leverage to explore potential future applications. This curiosity-driven investment is critical, because, without this innovation, we would likely devolve into a commoditization trap, as every brand would eventually catch up to incremental innovations. As Kaleeta McDade highlighted in Chapter 9, that happened rapidly in the early days of digital transformation, when the technology wasn't evolving as quickly as it could be implemented, but technology advancements rapidly reemerged with the improvements in web interfaces, mobile connectivity, and data and analytics.

PREDICTIONS SOMETIMES MISS THE MARK

Part of the reason that transformative investments remain the domain of these hypercapitalized companies is because several ideas miss the mark. For those who keep a finger on the pulse of the experience industry, it's well known that many innovations didn't succeed, often due to bad timing or simply due to misjudging the need and demand in the marketplace. This is a key lesson in Chapter 7: do not fear failure or you'll limit your ability to succeed. This is true with both incremental innovation and transformative innovation.

One of the most forward-thinking solutions that failed to gain traction was Google Glass, the AR-enabled wearable device designed to superimpose data and interaction functionality inside of transparent eyewear. Launched as a pilot in 2013 and rolled out at scale in 2014, Google Glass was a well thought out solution that seemed to meet a market need, as both employees and consumers demanded smarter wearable devices, more effective methods of interaction, and real-time access to situational data. Design studios and experience agencies, including my agency at the time, explored state-of-the-art possibilities, focusing primarily on business applications where data could be superimposed over real-world objects to assist an employee with completing a process. One notable pilot solution that my team created at the time allowed a hypothetical insurance adjuster to look at a building through their Google Glass device and instantly see known information about the building itself as well as the land it sits on, the geographic area it sits within, and buildings within close proximity. This could, theoretically, be managed and manipulated hands-free, allowing this employee to work on other tasks in parallel. It was a brilliant productivity solution. Other agencies and design groups came up with equally clever use cases and demonstrable utility was available everywhere.

Unfortunately, despite the utility, Google Glass didn't gain momentum. Subjective reviews declared that the form factor was viewed negatively, with wearers being called "gleeks" or even "glassholes," and the presentation of information and visuals within the peripheral vision of the wearer was considered too distracting. Fortunately, the product remains under development, with a more recent enterprise edition of the product released in 2019,[3] so the potential utility may still be realized. Google Glass also served as an inspiration for many recent augmented reality (AR)-enabled wearables being released by smaller, specialty vendors. My personal opinion is that this technology will eventually be adopted widely by the global population, once the population is ready for the solution (a lesson highlighted in Chapter 7).

Another forward-thinking innovation that ultimately fizzled was Apple's Newton, which preceded the iPad by 15 years. Complete with an integrated stylus, handwriting recognition, and a series of applications written for the proprietary operating system, the Newton was one of the original personal digital assistants. The Newton was unique in footprint and flexibility, and primarily designed to be a supplemental device for productivity, with a feature-rich calendar and to-do list manager, a contact database that could be synchronized with a desktop PC, a Notes application that allowed users to create small documents that had been typed or recognized from handwriting, and a free-form drawing app that could capture freehand sketches. The Newton gained early traction in the medical provider industry, as it was a convenient tool for capturing notes while performing rounds and interacting with patients.

Unfortunately for Apple, the Newton had relatively low market adoption, public failures of the handwriting recognition (which were satirized in *The Simpsons* TV show and the *Doonesbury* comic strip), and intense competition from the smaller-footprint, lower-price-point Palm Pilot, which likely was inspired by the Newton's capabilities. Due to the influence of Steve Jobs, the Newton project was shelved. It was not without dramatic impact, however, as the Newton was a primary inspiration behind the design of Apple's future touch and gesture devices, including the iPhone and the iPad.[4]

It's amusing to note that Gary Trudeau, the creator of the *Doonesbury* comic strip, is quoted in Mat Honan's 2013 *Wired* magazine article as saying that he decided to add a mythical failure of Apple Newton handwriting to his strip, because, to slightly paraphrase, the idea of replacing a perfectly good $5 notebook with a $700 computer seemed an easy target.[5] This shows that individual or group inability to see transformation potential can limit true progression in design and capability. It reminds me of a personal experience, back in the 1990s, when I met with a chief information officer from an international Fortune 100 company (who I will not name out of respect) to discuss Internet-enabled contact center solutions and the potential of seamless integration across virtual centers. We started discussing the emerging Internet in general, and he confidentially declared that "this whole Internet thing is nothing but hype. People don't want to work on computers – we're social beings, and nothing will ever replace face-to-face interactions." As you might expect, he was no longer employed by that company a year later, and the entire company was defunct within a few years.

EMERGING EXPERIENCE TRENDS

What are a few emerging trends that are worthy of some level of investigation and investment? The answer to this question requires some qualification, which is why I dedicated the previous section of this chapter to the discussion of failures. This qualification, which I share with all of my clients, is that it's important to recognize that predicting the future is an exercise in guessing. No one could guess that the Newton would fail but the iPad would be an overnight success. Google Glass seemed like the right solution at the right time, but it devolved into a slanderous term. Similarly, no one could guess that MySpace and Google+ would fail but Facebook would gather close to 3 billion monthly active users.[6] There are many other examples of absolutely brilliant technology – Magic Leap's augmented reality headset comes to mind – that haven't yet caught on even though these solutions were well designed, grounded in market research, and quite innovative and novel at the time of their release. So while the ideas and possibilities outlined in sections that follow represent real potential innovations, only time will tell if the timing and the market need align. There's no guarantee of results or returns from these investments. When your brand is evaluating an emerging experience trend, it's important to moderate the level of investment until your company's balance sheet will tolerate significant risk. As with incremental innovations, start with a controlled pilot and measure the results in the market. In parallel, measure the market sentiment to the transformative trend itself, and set threshold triggers that will lead you to continue investing or abandon the idea. This balance will ensure your brand experience remains novel without putting the company itself in a bad financial position.

With that qualifier in place, there are several areas that I strongly recommend my clients start to explore and to plan for as they consider the direction that customer experience will take in the future and the opportunity it presents for them. The rest of this chapter will examine these emerging experience trends.

AI-ENABLED CONVERSATIONAL INTERFACES

I believe that we are approaching the death of the basic request-response interface. Throughout the digital transformation era, most solutions were built with this concept in mind. Whether you're searching (enter the search query, receive results), exploring products and services (click on this link, see content related to the link), transacting (click this button, complete the transaction), or performing other functions, the paradigm is that you take a singular action and the application responds. Efficient design makes the path to a specific outcome more intuitive, so that individuals can navigate quickly through the experience, saving time and satisfying the modern customer. However, it still requires a path, and it requires continuous engagement from the individual with the application.

The evolution of digital assistants to incorporate voice interfaces and AI is an area of particular interest. Although IBM was the first to roll out a digital typewriter in the 1980s, with a vocabulary of 20,000 words, and the first digital assistant in the early 1990s, IBM Simon, the technology truly began taking hold after Apple launched Siri in 2010. Soon to follow were IBM's Watson, Microsoft's Cortana, Amazon's Alexa, Facebook's M, Google's G-Assistant, Alibaba's AliGenie, and Yandex's Alice.[7] The fast rollout is in itself a validation of the traction that voice interfaces have in the marketplace, but the reality is that the technology remains nascent. The true opportunity will present itself when these tools shift beyond simple transcription tools, and they're already beginning to do so. I text from my iPhone with voice far more frequently using voice than I do with the keyboard. In fact, AI-powered virtual assistants have gained significant traction in the last two years. According to Gartner's forecast for 2021, businesses will spend $3.5 billion on virtual personal assistants. By 2025, 50% of knowledge workers will use a virtual assistant on a daily basis, up from 2% in 2019. By 2023, Gartner predicts that 25% of employee interactions will be voice-based communications.[8] I maintain strong faith in Gartner's predictions, and this promotes the incrementality opportunity that virtual assistants offer to many brands.

The longer-term, big Innovation opportunity is in creating an AI-enabled conversational interface that maintains the context of the conversation across multiple requests. Often referred to as an intelligent assistant or bot, this interface will have the ability to learn over time, to customize responses to the profile and previous interactions with the individual, and to drive a process and resolution across channels and tasks.

Don't confuse this with the ubiquitous chatbot that's now available in so many web experiences and smartphone applications. These tools can be effective, but they need to be deployed properly, as they are limited in their intelligence (even with AI enablement) and typically follow a branching tree model. They are designed to accept simple inquiries, such as "What's my order status" or "How can I change my password," but not be used for sophisticated interactions. Once the question is asked and answered, the chatbot has lost context, and effectively is starting over from scratch.

I need to share an experience with a brand that tried to take their chatbot too far. I recently got caught in a chatbot trap when I was interacting with an airline I don't often fly, trying to change a flight. The website continued to return an error. While I have the top loyalty status with another airline, this trip was inside the borders of a foreign country, so the only status I had with them was the value given to the fare class of my ticket. Given that I had no status, I didn't want to be on hold for an extended period with the contact center, so I clicked the Help button on the website and was prompted to contact them via a WhatsApp-enabled chatbot. When I sent a message to the WhatsApp phone number, a chatbot interface responded, asking a series of six prescribed questions and then branching to four subquestions. When the app finally concluded that I was trying to change my flight, it provided a link to the website. When I responded that the website was returning an error, the chatbot said that it didn't understand my response and took me back to the main chat menu. Ultimately, I was forced to call into the contact center, where I waited on hold for over two hours, and was finally disconnected with a message that no agents were available to take my call and that they recommended that I contact them via WhatsApp. Fortunately for me, I finally reached a very helpful agent on Twitter who changed my flight, but imagine my perception and loyalty position with this airline going forward given that experience.

These are the inherent limitations of chatbots. AI-enabled conversational interfaces would be useful in both precommitment stages of the customer funnel, with the intelligent bot providing the ultimate convenience in guided selling and recommendations, while in parallel capturing your customer's needs for post-transaction service. This AI-enabled bot could follow up in real time with the customer, being fully interactive across channels. It has the potential to provide the ultimate in intimate experiences, effectively giving each customer a dedicated assistant who's available 24/7, engaging with the customer when they want, how they want, and at the pace that they want. As game-changing a concept as this is, the technology is going to be widely available fairly soon.

As an example of AI-enabled bot impact, imagine engaging with a commerce site that maintains a sophisticated conversational AI interface. When you access the site, or the app, using the channel that you desire, the assistant asks how they can help you. Perhaps you ask, "I'm looking for a gift for my sister. She tends to like brighter colors, and tries to keep up with the latest trends while equally wearing things that are popular for a woman in her 40s. Her birthday is in two weeks. What's available and what do you recommend?" The assistant, mimicking a human salesperson, would likely ask a clarifying question or two, confirming whether you're thinking of a specific article of clothing, such as a sweater, and might ask about size. Even more interesting, the assistant might ask you to search your phone for a couple of recent photos of your sister wearing different outfits, and upload them, which the AI tool could then scan and analyze to assess specific elements of style to emulate. The goal will be to gather enough information to understand the ask and the goal, and then marry that up with as much data as available to personalize the recommendation for maximum impact.

Once all necessary information is collected, the assistant could send recommendations to you over your preferred channel. Perhaps they're pushed to your smartphone browser or app, or if you prefer, they're sent to you as a text message or a WhatsApp message. Even more dynamically, they're sent to a virtualization interface that shows the product on an avatar, which can be rotated and viewed in three dimensions or even in simulated motion, giving you a better view of the product than can be gleaned from a static image. You can then ask questions, such as "Is the fabric itchy?" or "Has this been popular in my area?" continuing the conversation and the real-time interaction. You might decide that none of the products match your sister's style, and the assistant will happily look further for other options. Ultimately, you select your gift, and the assistant places the order on your behalf. If necessary, the assistant will capture a form of payment, confirm billing and shipping addresses, and offer multiple shipping options.

More interestingly and powerfully, the assistant will stay connected to you and your order throughout fulfillment. Rather than sending an e-mail or a text message with a tracking number, your assistant reaches out to you with a customized message at every stage of the fulfillment cycle. If anything is outside of the standard parameters of the order (the product hasn't shipped, delivery is delayed, etc.), the assistant will work with other systems to track down what is causing the delay and work to remediate it on your behalf. Once delivered, the assistant will follow up to ensure you're satisfied with the order, and be at the ready to initiate a return merchandise authorization (RMA) if that is necessary.

This is the type of service that only the ultra-rich would receive in the historical world of physical retail, mostly because it was impossible to scale. However, in the digital world, with the advancements in computing power, data analytics, artificial intelligence, and multibranching application logic, this experience could soon be available for the masses.

This is all hypothetical, and I could flesh out similar use cases for commercial banking, for insurance companies, for healthcare providers, for hospitality brands, and for virtually any industry. The tone and tenor of the dialogue can be designed to reflect your brand personality, but the potential of advanced AI-enabled chatbots reflects the ultimate ideal interface of the post-digital transformation – it saves time, it's novel, and it's humanized. Although the technology is not as sophisticated today as HAL in *2001: A Space Odyssey*, as Kit on *Knight Rider,* or even as the WOPR in *War Games*, the technology is evolving rapidly. My recommendation is to start now, embracing Gartner's prediction of virtual assistant adoption, and stand at the forefront of innovation as new capabilities emerge. Based on the level of adoption to date, the market is ready to make the shift, and will rapidly explore and embrace advancements that your brand introduces ahead of the overall market.

Tangential to this, but equally impactful in my view, is the approaching death of the keyboard. Reflecting on that statement as I type this paragraph, I realize how inefficient typing is as a means of word capture. Even though I can currently type at 70 words per minute with a 97% accuracy, per typing.com's student typing test (thank you to Mr. Bostwick, my ninth-grade typing teacher who started me on this path to typing efficiency), the average person types approximately 52 words per minute.[9] When you consider that English speakers can typically speak between 120 and 160 words per minute[10] or, on average, 3.5 times the speed of an average typist, it immediately becomes obvious how inefficient the keyboard is as a text input interface.

This is exacerbated further by the continuous shift from desktops and laptops to the smartphone. While I would never consider writing a book on a smartphone, people are using it for more detailed transcriptions. Surprisingly, the average typing speed doesn't decline quite as dramatically for the average typist – according to a 2019 study done by researchers from Aalto University in Finland and the University of Cambridge in the U.K., the average speed is 36.2 words per minute[11] – the rate of input is a dismal one-fifth as fast as speech would be.

It was rumored that Steve Jobs despised the keyboard, although, publicly, the most oft-referenced moment was when he dismantled a keyboard and professed that he hated function keys in particular. However, I believe that the frustration was rooted more in the realization that keyboards are inefficient for the most part.

As you consider the opportunity to implement AI-enabled chatbots and other forms of information capture (such as on a mobile device), consider the possibility of voice capture and transmission. More and more, people prefer to use voice transcription, and adoption is outsized with Millennials and Generation Z, who have not grown up in a world of typewriters and word processors. Fortunately, most devices, including popular smartphone models, laptop models, and streaming service devices, already provide a voice interface, so the amount of effort necessary to extend this to your brand experience should be relatively minimal.

AUGMENTED REALITY

Another trend that I believe is worthy of investigation and investment is augmented reality (AR). Augmented reality is a solution that superimposes visuals over a physical image. It's actively in use today, mainly through the cameras on handheld smartphones or tablets. One popular example is IKEA's Place application, a furniture visualization tool that inserts an IKEA product into the room. As you walk around the room with your smartphone or tablet, you can see the piece from different angles. As of 2020, with the studio mode available on the new iPad Pro, the application is able to analyze more detailed three-dimensional depth information to create an even more realistic image. In fact, if you desire, you can turn on and off virtual lights to see how they change the scene. If you haven't used it, I'd recommend you explore it, as it's one of the best examples of the potential of AR. Another well-formed and popular example is Ulta Beauty's GLAMlab, a virtual product trial application, which again uses the phone or tablet's camera to superimpose products directly on a person, allowing the individual to change their hair color, try various products, and evaluate the look. Per Ulta Beauty's application description, all textures, colors, and finishes are true to life. There are other examples in other industries, but AR certainly tilts heavily toward retail or direct-to-consumer brands that are interested in seeing the application of the product to a physical environment. Clever brands are bringing AR into the store itself, implementing a "magic mirror" functionality that provides the same capability on a larger screen, often with higher fidelity. This is a good application of the technology that meets a defined need, but it's far from transformative.

True transformative innovation will, as discussed earlier in this chapter, involve some form of visual wearable that allows us to interact with augmented reality without having to hover a smartphone camera and interact with a screen. Recognizing that Google already made a big bet in this area with Google Glass, and equally recognizing that several niche vendors have been investing in this capability without traction beyond specific use cases, my point of view is that AR will have its watershed moment in the near future, with accelerated adoption and, eventually, a shift away from two-dimensional browser and smartphone interfaces.

What will drive this adoption? I believe primarily business applications, such as the insurance adjuster application that my studio put together with Google Glass. The opportunity for productivity gains is significant. Facial recognition applications, within the reasonable boundaries of privacy rules, are another application. Visual notifications, likely on the periphery of the visual field, will allow people to remain engaged with others without the awkward distraction of the continuously vibrating smartphone. Product detail could be super-imposed in the visual field as the individual browses a store, and managers can scan a restaurant to identify how best to optimize cus-tomer seating against their current waitstaff assignments. Although adoption, in my view, will be driven by internal enterprise applica-tions, the adoption will then move to the front office and, eventually, brand experience opportunities will emerge. Enterprise-to-consumer progression is the path that other technologies, including the personal computer, followed, so it's not an uncommon evolution.

As an example, imagine enterprise augmented reality employed in a manufacturing plant. As each individual on the manufacturing line completes their task, their visual wearable could evaluate and analyze the product, confirming that the task was performed prop-erly, confirming that dimensions are within standard parameters, and confirming that there are no anomalies at that stage. The application would continue to progress with the product, dramatically reducing quality issues for the final product.

As another example, imagine augmented reality employed in a healthcare provider environment. Doctors and nurses can have patient data, diagnostics, and prescribed actions readily available in their visual field, eliminating the need to turn away from the patient to the nearby computer and having to log into Epic, Cerner, or others to pull this data. As the patient describes their current state, or as the doctor or nurse completes their evaluation, voice assistants or gesture interfaces could update the patient profile in real-time and prompt for suggested actions. It would improve the patient expe-rience while, equally, improving the doctor and nurse experience, particularly in time constrained situations such as hospital rounds.

Speaking of interfaces, just as conversational interfaces will be enhanced by AI-enabled voice assistants, augmented reality will be enhanced by gesture interfaces. Made popular by the movie *Minority Report*, where characters gesture dramatically to manipulate transparent AR interfaces, future experiences will incorporate gestures as a form of navigation. This will be particularly useful in environments where voice assistants aren't practical. If you're sitting in a library or a movie theater, and you need to engage with an application, you won't be inclined to start speaking to your device. Gestures are normal and natural and can be small or large in motion, allowing them to be applied to several environments. Apple has again pioneered the gesture interface with the swipe, and it's now extended to a range of devices, but soon these gestures will not require physical touch of the device. Instead, it will be detected by the AR scanner, and will interact directly with the visual display field.

To be clear, I don't believe that we'll devolve into a society where everyone is wandering around swinging their arms wildly in the air. Instead, controlled gestures can and likely will become a powerful navigational method to employ that will further humanize brand experiences. Investing in what's available today and positioning your experiences to take advantage of advanced augmented reality solutions as they are introduced may be a worthwhile investment to make.

THE METAVERSE AND NFTs

The final experience trend, and the one that offers the highest potential for generational transformation, is the metaverse. Metaverse is a term that gained significant momentum in 2021, when Mark Zuckerberg, founder and CEO of Meta (Facebook) made it the topic of his keynote speech at Connect 2021, and now it's a term that seems to dominate technology and financial conversations, news releases, and investment strategies.

So what exactly is the metaverse? It's more of a concept than a physical object. *Wired* magazine articulated this well in their November, 2021 article, where Eric Ravenscraft explains that the concept of the metaverse embraces two concepts: An immersive, interactive experience and a digital economy.[12]

The metaverse experience is best described as a set of virtual worlds, most often accessed through a browser, smartphone, or gaming console but now expanding to include virtual reality (VR) and augmented reality (AR) interfaces. Within the virtual world, the individual is presented as an avatar, which is a digital representation of the person, and the limits of avatar design tend to be quite open, allowing for unique expressions of individuality. Perhaps most interestingly, these virtual worlds continue to exist and operate even when the individual isn't online; these worlds are an alternative, technology-enabled space where people interact, engage, and congregate over time, regardless of who is actually participating. There are many examples of virtual worlds, with some of the most popular at the time of this writing including Fortnite, Decentraland, and The Sandbox.

Most of these worlds are grounded in the concept of gaming, but the game itself has been eclipsed by the experiences offered within the game. Epic Games' Fortnite, for example, hosted multiple concerts in 2021, including the popular acts of Travis Scott and Marshmello, but the most notable was Ariana Grande's virtual concert that drew over 27.7 million unique users. It is estimated that she earned over $20 million for the concert.[13] Similarly, Snoop Dogg purchased a virtual plot of land in The Sandbox, which is described as a "virtual metaverse world that allows users to play games within a game."[14] This led multiple high-net-worth individuals to purchase neighboring plots of virtual land in The Sandbox, next to Snoop Dogg's, for between $350,000 and $450,000.[15] Clearly, this is no longer just a game, and the experiential element of these virtual metaverse worlds are becoming the draw that are bringing people in.

However, as Ravenscraft explains in his *Wired* article, the concept of the metaverse is more than just an experience; it's also a unique digital economy with, suddenly, significant potential. This is reflected in Ariana Grande's concert in Fortnite and the virtual land transactions next to Snoop Dogg in The Sandbox. In fact, as of this book's writing in 2022, individuals and brands are investing significant money to secure virtual real estate within the most popular metaversian worlds. (The Sandbox tweeted in November 2021 that over 165 celebrity and brand partners have purchased land.[16]) However, this economy doesn't only engage in large transactions; in the various instantiations of the metaverse, users can create, buy, and sell goods. People are investing in their avatar's appearance, buying exclusive digital products sold by brands ranging from Ralph Lauren to Nike to Gucci. People are buying access to events, such as

Snoop Dogg's party palace, and people are buying experiences, such as drinking a virtual beer while playing virtual darts at the Miller Lite Tavern in Decentraland.[17]

The complexity of this simple description reflects the complexity of the term itself. As Ravenscraft says in his article, trying to describe the metaverse today is like trying to describe the Internet in the 1970s. The foundation is there, but there's so much still to be defined, that much of this early engagement remains speculative.[18]

Some people are referring to the metaverse as Web 3.0, or the third version of the Internet. To try and simplify this third version further, the metaverse is envisioned as a collection of virtual reality worlds that we can interact in and move around in a similar fashion to the real world. We can create a virtual avatar to "live" in this virtual world, and we can buy and sell virtual goods, including virtual land with virtual houses, virtual clothing, virtual food and drinks, and virtual art. Many of these virtual items are call non-fungible tokens, or NFTs, which are described in far greater detail later in this section.

The idea of the metaverse, and the term itself, can be traced back to the early 1990s, when it was used in Neal Stephenson's 1992 novel *Snow Crash*.[19] Following the pattern of science fiction predicting the future, Stephenson's vision for a virtual reality-fueled existence was surprisingly spot on. He envisioned a three-dimensional virtual world that would be accessed by goggles, that would be fully interactive, and that would allow for customization of the avatar.

Much more notable is the continued success of Second Life, which launched in 2003. Second Life, for those not familiar, is an online experience – a virtual world – where users create an avatar, navigate virtualized real-world environments, and interact with other avatars representing people from across the world. Fundamentally, this is the concept of the metaverse. It showed the potential of virtual interaction and, perhaps more importantly, it demonstrated that the metaverse can be monetized. Within Second Life there are free accounts and paid accounts, and those that engage are inclined to pay the recurring fee. But perhaps more interesting, these same users are willing to pay for virtual land and virtual experiences. This opens up a world of possibility and potential, and this lays the foundation for the future of the metaverse, where we're seeing the early stages of the same investments as outlined next.

While Second Life, like many digital experiences launched in the early aughts, has declined in popularity, it has remained relevant for many dedicated users. Linden Labs, the parent company behind Second Life, published an infographic in 2013 that professed an active user base of more than 1 million, with 36 million accounts created in the first 10 years. In 2021 the metric had shifted to average daily visitors, which is listed at 200,000 per day, but most likely the user distribution changes by the day, which would increase the average user count to be higher. Given that it's a worldwide user base – one current report shows only 50% of the active user base being in the United States – this is a small adoption rate, but it's an active and engaged one. This is a community that meets in virtual coffee shops, shops in virtual stores, works out in virtual gyms, and spends their evening dancing in virtual clubs. There are virtual marriages, with wedding venues, carriage rides, live vendors, and even photogenic spots in the virtual world. People are investing in their virtual houses, building virtual storefronts, and operating within the society as if it were a real world. While adoption is low, this behavior shows that a shift to virtualized societies is a possibility, at least as an escape for real life.

Significant acceleration of the metaverse as a concept occurred in 2021. Mark Zuckerberg announced the change in name from Facebook to Meta, publicly setting a strategy for the company that will focus on the development, and capitalization of the virtual reality movement. Other companies have started to invest in this area, including most notably Alphabet, Apple, and Microsoft, but Zuckerberg has completely shifted his company's business strategy and name to the metaverse opportunity. He did this for good reason, as Facebook is clearly a brand in decline as social media shifts rapidly to other platforms, and, more excitedly, current estimates forecast that the metaverse represents a $1 trillion revenue.[20] Today most metaverse environments are still accessed via two-dimensional browsers or game consoles, but Zuckerberg's hope is that it will shift to virtual realities. My guess is that it will likely evolve into a combination of augmented reality and browser/smartphone, with virtual reality being, primarily, the interface of younger gamers who are more willing to engage in a fully immersive environment. Regardless of the interface used for access, the metaverse trend does appear to have serious potential.

Another development propelling metaverse momentum in 2021 was that the creation and sale of NFTs hit the mainstream market. NFTs were first created in 2014 when digital artist Kevin McCoy minted a pixelated octagon filled with different shapes that pulse in a hypnotic way.[21] He named it Quantum. NFTs are digital assets that are created, bought, and sold on a free market, with all transaction details and ownership specifics documented on a blockchain. The indelible records on the blockchain ensure that all characteristics of an NFT are documented, reducing the risk of counterfeiting and fraud (this is why the assets are non-fungible). Almost exclusively, NFTs are purchased with cryptocurrency, with Etherium currently emerging as a standard.

If you don't understand cryptocurrency or blockchain technology at a level that allows the preceding paragraph to make sense, don't be concerned. You don't need to know all the lingo and jargon that goes along with NFTs to grasp the basic concept of NFTs or the metaverse, so you can investigate the underlying terminology at another time. What's important to understand is that the foundation for buying, selling, and owning NFTs standardized between 2014 and 2020, with the actual buying and selling primarily limited to virtual gaming environments.

That changed dramatically in 2021. Total NFT sales in 2020 were reported to be between $100 million and $340 million, depending on the source, whereas 2021 reported sales of $22 billion, according to *The Guardian*.[22] The original Quantum NFT that started it all sold at a Sotheby's digital auction in November 2021 for over $1.4 million.[23] People started buying virtual real estate at record levels, with three investors each spending over $400,000 for a parcel of virtual land next to entertainer Snoop Dogg's virtual property. Another investor purchased a virtual plot for $2.4 million, and yet another investor spent $650,000 on a virtual mega yacht.[24] All of these transactions are completed with cryptocurrency but the cryptocurrency transactions are grounded in cash valuations, which represents a true opportunity for your brand.

Early adopters, such as Gucci and Coca-Cola, are capitalizing on this NFT frenzy by introducing limited edition digital assets. Gucci's first foray into the NFT world, which drew inspiration from Gucci's most recent film, *Gucci Aria,* raised $25,000 for the brand at auction. Coca-Cola introduced their first NFT in August, with the proceeds benefiting the Special Olympics. They hosted a virtual "can-top" party in Decentraland, a virtual metaverse, on International Friendship Day (July 30, 2021), featuring music, giveaways and a first look at the Friendship Box NFT. Additionally, representatives from Coca-Cola and a range of metaverse organizations, including Tafi, OpenSea, and Decentraland Foundation, hosted a live AMA (Ask Me Anything) chat on Decentraland's Discord Channel to discuss the Coca-Cola Friendship Box NFT collaboration and what it means for the metaverse.[25]

Oana Vlad, global senior brand director of Coca-Cola Trademark, is quoted in Coca-Cola's press release, saying, "These activations added credibility and authenticity to the experience. They helped create a strong buzz both in the crypto community and with business, lifestyle and tech media, and also helped bring new, young audiences to our Coke Trademark social media channels." Overall, this was a huge success. The Coca-Cola Friendship NFT included a virtual vintage Coca-Cola cooler with dynamic motion and illumination featuring three other NFTs inside: a custom-designed Coca-Cola Bubble Jacket to be worn in the Decentraland 3D virtual reality platform, a Sound Visualizer illustrating the recognizable sonics of enjoying a Coca-Cola, and a Coca-Cola Friendship Card with refreshed artwork from 1948. The Coca-Cola Friendship NFT was auctioned off for over $575,000. The winning bidder also received a real-life, fully stocked Coca-Cola refrigerator.[26]

You will recall in Chapter 5, Selling Experiences, Not Products, that I mentioned that Nike and Adidas also have started exploring the potential of NFTs in the metaverse. Nike announced in December 2021 that they purchased RTFKT Studios, a digital visualization agency that Nike says "leverages cutting edge innovation to deliver next generation collectibles that merge culture and gaming."[27] RTFKT claims that in February 2021 a collaboration with teenage artist FEWOCiOUS to sell real sneakers paired with virtual ones managed to sell over 600 shoe pairs and NFTs together in just seven minutes, generating $3.1 million.[28] Nike recognizes that they need to be positioned to capture this future opportunity, quoting John Donahoe, president and CEO of Nike, Inc. in their press release: "This acquisition is another step that accelerates Nike's digital transformation and allows us to serve athletes and creators at the intersection of sport, creativity, gaming, and culture. We're acquiring a very talented team of creators with an authentic and connected brand. Our plan is to invest in the RTFKT brand, serve and grow their innovative and creative community and extend Nike's digital footprint and capabilities."[29]

Adidas, not to be outdone, announced a limited-edition launch of 30,000 Adidas Originals NFTs in November 2021 in collaboration with Bored Ape Yacht Club, who was one of the most successful NFT producers this year. The NFTs sold out in less than a second, and Adidas earned $23.4 million in the event. Adidas employed an exclusivity strategy with secretive and exclusive drip marketing on social media channels, which added to both the anticipation and the value of the event, likely contributing to the outcome.

The examples of these brands – and there are many others that could be highlighted – are impressive and should be applauded. They embrace the idea of innovation and novelty in the customer experience, extending that experience into this emerging world of virtual reality and non-fungible tokens while holding to the vision and strategy of their brands. However, these are tactical activities that only are touching on the fringes of this potential emerging opportunity, which is to be expected given the metaverse is still very much in the nascent stages. It will likely be several years before the metaverse reaches the mainstream and, like the Internet and the associated digital transformation before it, it most likely will be incremental, progressive, and, at times, a turbulent evolution.

To be clear, there are no guarantees that the metaverse concept will take off. The current NFT investment spike has indications of being an irrational bubble, although only time will show whether that's the case or if this is a trend to stay. I am not going to follow the example of my CIO client in the 1990s who told me that the Internet is a fad; I state with conviction that a form of metaverse interaction will take root and become part of our global society. I equally caution, however, that the broad nature of the metaverse expansion – pun intended – opens up the possibility of it moving in almost limitless directions. If you are looking for parallels in recent history, reflect on the collective stories of CompuServe, AOL, and Yahoo! in the early days of digital. They all reflected great early-stage ideas that were trapped in an evolutionary branch of digital that ultimately went extinct. Darwin's discoveries apply to digital transformation and post-digital transformation equally, and at this time we don't yet know which concepts will survive.

The smart move is to begin conservatively investing in the metaverse concept now, likely through the NFT craze that is sweeping the space, for if this platform does truly expand and consumers and business buyers begin interacting in this virtual world, you need to be ready to build an experience that mirrors your brand identity. In many ways, this will be the ultimate fusion of physical and digital experiences given that, while this is entirely a digital platform, it will be populated by real people together with AI-driven conversational interfaces that will be fueling everything from brand awareness to transaction to servicing, culminating in brand loyalty. It's entirely possible that the metaverse will become a primary method of brand interaction, effectively replacing current methods – desktops, laptops, smart tablets, and smart phones – in their entirety in 10 years, with individuals tapping into the metaverse using unobtrusive visual and audio wearables. It brings together the best of the social experience of shopping with friends, complete with coffee and lunch breaks, along with the ultimate convenience of online commerce. It provides the inherent connectivity and focus of in-person meetings without the hours of travel delays and extensive costs of physically coming together for every meeting. It provides an opportunity for person-to-person servicing at scale with individual servicers potentially being able to service a number of clients in parallel, supported by highly evolved AI-enabled chat bots. We don't necessarily have to strap on full virtual reality goggles as we do today – the technology will inevitably evolve and improve and well-funded companies are exploring the art of possible. When you reflect on what we've introduced over the past 25 years, it's not a stretch to imagine true revolutions in experience, in the next 10–15 years, and the brand experience opportunities that it will bring.

CHAPTER 11

Where You Should Begin

Chapters 4 through 9 explored six strategies to align your experience with your brand strategy and Chapter 10 examined several emerging trends that you should be thinking of when defining your future brand experience. The natural question to ask now is, "Where should I begin?" It can be a bit overwhelming to consider the complexity of your enterprise brand strategy, the equal complexity of the markets within which your brand operates, and finally the alignment of both of them with the initiatives that will generate the best impact and return in both the short and the long term. Most often, the best place to begin is with an assessment. I often tell my clients that the approach to assessments is a series of threes.

THREE APPROACHES TO ASSESSMENTS

There is always a reason to evaluate your experiences and look for opportunities to improve.

I've worked with a lot of organizations, and depending on their focus and needs, the practical approaches to assessments generally fall into three broad categories. All three of these approaches are valid and accretive to engagement and financial metrics.

I have worked with brands in multiple industries that were seeing a clear and measured negative result in a particular business, geography, customer segment, or channel, and the initial focus of the assessment is on the combination of experience touchpoints that service the area in decline. A negative result doesn't necessarily mean negative growth or high rates of defection – it could be an increase in call-handling costs in the call center, a reduction in visit rates to the primary website, or an announcement by a competitor that they are introducing a new experience strategy that is gaining positive attention in the market. Regardless, if there's an acute need, there are obvious gains in focusing on that area and building the foundation of an experience modernization strategy around improving that individual performance metric.

Additionally, I have worked with more proactive enterprises that recognize that they need to keep a continuous finger on the pulse of the effectiveness and relevance of their experiences across channels, and they need to make a broader assessment to find the acute need. This type of broader market scan can be completed quite efficiently and can quickly lead to a roadmap of initiatives that can be implemented in successive order, with clear measurements of success defined to keep the team grounded to quantifiable goals.

Finally, I've worked with truly visionary enterprises that leverage the experience assessment to identify opportunities to differentiate their brand through new, novel, innovative, time-saving experiences, engaging with their customers at a deeper level at every stage of the customer journey, separating themselves from their competitors. The example brands outlined in this book all fall into this category, which is why their stories, and the lessons gleaned from them, are so compelling.

THREE PREREQUISITES FOR ASSESSMENTS

Before you start with your assessment, there are three prerequisites that must be in place.

First and foremost, ensure that you have your latest identity guidelines for your brand, both to understand the brand strategy and the brand tone and messaging. This will allow you to effectively map your experiences to your overall brand voice. Sit down with the brand strategy team to thoroughly understand the proposition, voice, and personality of the brand.

Second you need a market analysis of your customers and prospective customers. If a relatively recent market segmentation study, identifying the motivations, needs and emotional triggers of detailed personas within segments, isn't available, this needs to be completed. This can be wide ranging or very specific, depending on the question that you're trying to solve. but for the initial stages of an assessment, specific is usually better than general, because the effort increases and the level of granularity decreases as you broaden the scope. If you don't have the time or budget to complete a full investment, there are agencies and analyst groups that can rapidly compile general insights of target markets, but if possible, a rapid survey and associated analysis is incredibly valuable, as understanding your market and the triggers that drive market behavior is key to any experience effort. Without this, you are relying on your instincts and, effectively, shooting into the dark with your planned improvements.

Finally, you need an understanding of the customer journey – the primary path that a customer takes through awareness, education and investigation, transaction, servicing, and loyalty. This is often referred to as the happy path, and it's highly probable that it already exists somewhere in the organization. If not, it can be built quickly. There may be some discussion of deviations from the happy path that are germane to the assessment itself, and it's possible that there are multiple happy paths to consider as the journey is evaluated across channels. However, most important is to build a foundational understanding, as it will ground much of the decisioning and analysis. As I often advise my clients, don't let perfect be the enemy of good. A general view of the journey will be sufficient for your initial assessment, and the journey itself can be continuously updated as you complete the initial assessment and, further, as you begin adjusting elements of the experience.

THREE AREAS OF ASSESSMENTS

With the three prerequisites from the previous section in hand, the assessment should address three specific areas.

For the first area of assessment, evaluate whether the channels, and the touchpoints within each channel, are properly expressing your brand. This is often done through a process known as an outside-in or top-down heuristic or, alternatively, as an experience teardown. Different agencies and consultancies will have their own vocabulary, but the process and the objectives are the same. This is a bit of a manual approach; user experience specialists from your team, or a digital agency partner, emulate your customer's experience by following the happy path from initial engagement through commitment and through to loyalty. They'll test multiple iterations of the happy path, for, as we discussed at length throughout this book, there are multiple paths of discovery and awareness. Exploring initial awareness paths set the context for the overall brand tone of the experience. These paths will likely land in different points across the physical and digital experience, so this process needs to be iterated several times to gain a complete understanding. For brands with a physical experience, running a secret shopper process, a silent observer process, or a series of interviews – ideally of both employees and customers – at key locations will provide the insight needed.

Beyond this direct evaluation of the experience, it's also valuable to scan social and web channels to complete a sentiment analysis of the brand. This is often done using digital listening tools that identify relevant web and social media posts, capturing and algorithmically evaluating the sentiment being expressed. As with any machine learning technology, the automated evaluation is not perfect or fully accurate, but it rapidly accelerates what would otherwise by a painfully manual process. There are many tools available in the marketplace offering this functionality and while I have my personal favorites, I'll abstain from providing recommendations here. I would work with your digital agency or consulting partner to select a tool that works best for your brand's needs.

It's also possible to leverage standard sentiment metrics such as net promoter score (NPS) or customer satisfaction (CSAT) to gain greater insight into perception of the brand, but these are broader measurements of brand loyalty and product satisfaction, and not specific to the brand voice, tone, and alignment to brand strategy. I would remain limited in the use of these measurement methodologies for this specific evaluation.

This exercise may sound extensive, but with an experienced set of practitioners, it can be completed over a span of weeks, drawing significant insights, and a prioritized roadmap of improvements, in a relatively short period of time.

The second area of assessment is the effectiveness of your experiences in meeting your customer's needs and expectations. This can and should be completed partially through the same heuristic process described earlier, but the evaluation is focused on completely different elements of the experience. Working methodically through the personas defined in the market assessment, the user experience specialist will assess not only whether the experience meets the specific need, but how effectively and clearly the need is met. Metrics such as click paths, page load speed, navigation efficiency, and interface layout will influence this assessment. Content and visualizations will be evaluated against known emotional triggers, in both the physical and digital environments. The same sentiment analysis tools and in-store interviews will provide real-time perspective on whether the expectations and needs are being met.

Adding to this, the team should complete a comprehensive review of analytics across digital channels, evaluating where visitors are engaging, the volume of engagement, and then the progressive metrics through the journey. With the imminent "death of the cookie," which will eliminate the cross-page tracking, and the asynchronous nature of customer engagement today – they may engage with the website, disengage, run a search, engage with another page, disengage, download the mobile app, link out to a social post, and ultimately end up in a physical location – running metrics to define a specific customer journey is becoming impossible, but engagement spikes and degradations will provide insight into what's working and what's not working. Again, this evaluation collectively will lead to a prioritized roadmap of initiatives, which can be reconciled together with the brand voice roadmap to create a prioritized set of initiatives and improvements.

Finally, the third area of assessment should measure the effectiveness of your brand experience in progressing your customer through their journey. The granularity, and overall accuracy, of this assessment will vary depending on the depth of data that you currently collect on prospective and existing customers and the depth of activity data across physical and digital channels. Most enterprise digital experiences have basic metrics that track the number of unique visits, unique opens, and unique source paths. Transactions can be measured both online and in store to measure trending, and then, when appropriate, recurrence and share of wallet growth of existing customers can be measured through the loyalty program. The objective is to find notable drop-offs at stages of the journey, which will lead to additional prioritizations on the roadmap.

AGILE EXPERIENCE INNOVATION

Once the roadmap is finished, the next action is to establish a set of Agile-based operating teams to address the documented actions. These teams should focus on both experience improvement and development – new experience innovation – and experience operations across the funnel.

The former focuses on the continuous improvement and modernization of every touchpoint, both physical and digital, taking in inputs from customers, from employees, from automated listening channels, and from the data itself. The roadmap should be converted into a backlog of initiatives, which are then broken down into tasks and rapid, iterative releases. Based on the market response, this backlog will continue to evolve, and priorities will change. Essentially, the market response will guide the prioritization and release schedule, and the innovation engine will be sparked.

The latter focuses on proactive communications to the market, both to prospective and existing customers. With an unprecedented range of channels available for communication, including physical, e-mail, social, notification, streaming services, and others, the opportunity to progress a proactive discussion with customers across the funnel has never been richer, and it requires a test-and-learn, Agile-based approach to determine what the best method of communication is by segment and by persona. Again, as discussed earlier, the response data will help direct the initiatives and the approach will continuously evolve with the market need.

For those not familiar with Agile methodologies, the fundamental tenets include working to create a minimum viable product, or MVP, and testing that product in the market, collecting real-time feedback through direct communication and through analytics and responding to that market response to continuously refine the solution. Agile teams work in close collaboration with continuous communication, meeting daily in a stand-up where they review the progress from the previous day and the tasks for the current day. Critical decisions are made within the team guided by the input of a product owner, who has ultimate accountability for the business requirements of the solution being developed, and, depending on whether the team is following Scrum or Kanban, there are different methodologies for managing the tasks and overall scope of the project.

That's a very quick and high-level description of Agile methodologies, and if this is not an approach that your organization actively employs, I would strongly encourage your team to engage with an Agile coach who can help structure team roles and train the team on the ceremonies and processes that define the methodology. Agencies, consultancies, and direct-hire experts can bring this insight and understanding to your teams. It can take time to grow comfortable with the approach, but the benefit of Agile is that it's designed for speed and efficiency, prioritizing market testing over internal design and iterative development over full solution development. For experience improvements, this is a natural fit, as the Agile approach encourages innovation and creative exploration while it, equally, allows the organization to roll back changes that don't have the desired brand impact.

Depending on your organization's operating structure and culture, this may be a common approach, or it may be a dramatic shift in thinking. Fortunately, for those organizations that are not naturally inclined to adopt Agile principles, there are several hybrid models that can provide some of the benefits of the methodology. Adopting as much of Agile principles as the organization allows will improve returns for certain, so I encourage you to help your organization stretch themselves as much as possible.

The key is to recognize that your brand experience can never be static, as the moment you stop evolving your experiences, your brand starts descending into antiquity and irrelevance. Your market and your customer will continuously evolve, and the approaches and technology that they use to engage with you will continue to improve. The pace of change that we experienced during the digital transformation age will likely feel slow in comparison with what is coming in this newly emerging post-digital transformation age, and those brands that continue to evolve their experiences in response to the market, while remaining true to the brand's purpose, vision, and voice, will emerge from this era stronger than ever. With that, good luck, and I look forward to engaging with your brand in whatever environment the market takes us over the next several years!

Notes

INTRODUCTION

1. Charles Alexander, *Breaking the Slump: Baseball in the Depression Era* (New York: Columbia University Press, 2002), pp. 41–42. Citation provided by Wikipedia and not independently confirmed by author.
2. "IRP Phase I Air Force Plants Nos 28+29" (pdf). Air Force Engineering Services Center, June 1984, p. 27.

CHAPTER 1: A FAR TOO BRIEF HISTORY OF BRAND STRATEGY

1. https://www.entrepreneur.com/encyclopedia/branding
2. Ibid.
3. https://www.atticpaper.com/proddetail.php?prod=1905-ford-model-b-and-c-ad
4. https://www.history.com/topics/inventions/model-t
5. https://www.businessinsider.com/how-pan-am-went-from-pioneering-air-travel-to-bankruptcy-2020-2
6. Ibid.
7. https://history.state.gov/milestones/1969-1976/oil-embargo
8. https://www.britannica.com/topic/Disney-Company
9. https://guestexperiencedesign.com/at-disney-its-all-about-the-experience/
10. https://www.forbes.com/sites/blakemorgan/2020/01/23/5-lessons-from-disneys-magical-customer-experience/?sh=3b6215577555

CHAPTER 2: THE DAWN OF DIGITAL

1. https://www.linkedin.com/pulse/since-2000-52-companies-fortune-500-have-vanished-sam-tanham/
2. https://www.imdb.com/title/tt2543312/
3. https://www.pewresearch.org/internet/2007/06/21/the-internet-circa-1998/
4. https://oko.uk/blog/the-history-of-online-advertising
5. https://www.britannica.com/topic/Yahoo-Inc
6. https://montulli.blogspot.com/2013/05/the-reasoning-behind-web-cookies.html
7. https://www.smartinsights.com/email-marketing/email-communications-strategy/email-marketing-evolution/
8. https://www.wired.com/1996/12/the-spam-to-end-all-spams-is-coming/
9. https://www.statista.com/statistics/420400/spam-email-traffic-share-annual/

CHAPTER 3: FOCUSING ON THE MODERN CONSUMER

1. https://tvquot.es/modern-family/pilot/
2. https://equalman.com/statistics-show-social-media-is-bigger-than-you-think/
3. https://socialnomics.net/2013/01/01/social-media-video-2013/
4. https://www.oberlo.com/blog/google-search-statistics
5. https://chainstoreage.com/study-most-product-searches-begin-amazon
6. https://ecommercenews.eu/nearly-half-of-product-searches-start-on-marketplace/

CHAPTER 4: BELIEVING IN YOUR BRAND AND REDEFINING YOUR STRATEGY

1. https://www.britannica.com/topic/Starbucks
2. https://www.starbucks.com/about-us/
3. https://designbro.com/blog/industry-thoughts/starbucks-logo-meaning/

4. https://www.britannica.com/topic/Starbucks
5. https://www.starbucks.com/about-us/
6. https://ivypanda.com/essays/starbucks-company-decline-and-transformation/
7. Ibid.
8. https://capgemini.com/consulting/wp-content/uploads/sites/30/2017/08/starbucks.pdf
9. https://www.entrepreneur.com/article/229299
10. https://datascience.foundation/datatalk/retail-chains-starbucks-data-analytics-and-business-intelligence
11. https://digital.hbs.edu/platform-rctom/submission/digitizing-the-starbucks-experience/
12. https://www.entrepreneur.com/article/229299
13. Ibid.

CHAPTER 5: SELLING EXPERIENCES, NOT PRODUCTS

1. https://www.consumerwatchdog.org/privacy-technology/how-google-and-amazon-are-spying-you
2. https://en.wikipedia.org/wiki/Adidas
3. Ibid.
4. https://en.wikipedia.org/wiki/Nike,_Inc.
5. https://en.wikipedia.org/wiki/Nike_Cortez
6. https://www.gameplan-a.com/2021/08/the-history-of-adidas-a-background-of-collaboration-and-innovation/
7. Ibid.
8. Ibid.
9. https://www.washingtonpost.com/archive/business/1998/01/18/nikes-downward-swoosh/c2842d6c-7017-4f67-a673-daec369e0252/
10. https://mashable.com/archive/nike-social-media
11. https://ecommercedb.com/en/store/nike.com
12. https://mashable.com/archive/nike-social-media
13. Ibid.
14. https://news.nike.com/news/nike-and-google-create-global-online-community-for-football
15. Ibid.

16. https://www.givemesport.com/1677222-ronaldinhos-nike-advert-doing-the-crossbar-challenge-was-it-fake
17. https://news.nike.com/news/nike-soho-first-look
18. https://www.statista.com/statistics/895136/footwear-market-share-of-nike-and-adidas-by-region/
19. https://www.retaildive.com/news/nike-doubles-down-on-localization-with-nike-rise-concept/604819/
20. Ibid.
21. Ibid.
22. Ibid.
23. Ibid.
24. Ibid.
25. Ibid.
26. Ibid.

CHAPTER 6: TIME IS THE NEW CURRENCY – ANTICIPATING WITHOUT BEING INVASIVE

1. https://opher-ganel.medium.com/time-is-money-doesnt-mean-what-you-think-it-means-ba993723819c
2. https://www.nytimes.com/2021/08/17/technology/amazon-walmart.html
3. https://www.britannica.com/topic/Amazoncom
4. Jeffrey P. Bezos, 1997 Letter to Shareholders (from the 1997 Annual Report).
5. https://www.britannica.com/topic/Amazoncom
6. https://www.dynamicyield.com/files/ebooks/DY-Book-Amazon.pdf
7. https://etaileast.wbresearch.com/blog/panera-bread-omnichannel-strategy
8. https://www.qsrmagazine.com/outside-insights/case-digital-ordering-quick-service
9. https://fortune.com/2014/03/27/with-digital-ordering-panera-makes-a-big-bet-on-tech/
10. Ibid.

11. https://www.panerabread.com/content/dam/panerabread/documents/press/2014/panera-unveils-panera-2.0.pdf
12. https://hospitalitytech.com/digital-demands-influence-paneras-next-gen-store-design
13. Ibid.
14. Ibid.

CHAPTER 7: FINDING A NOVEL APPROACH TO SOLVING A MARKET NEED

1. https://blog.logomyway.com/lululemon-logo-and-history/
2. https://info.lululemon.com/about/our-story/history
3. https://archive.canadianbusiness.com/business-strategy/toned-and-ready-lululemon-transitions/
4. https://risnews.com/lululemon-outlines-digital-initiatives
5. https://retail-insider.com/retail-insider/2014/12/lululemon-2/
6. Ibid.
7. https://www.instyle.com/beauty/lululemon-lab-concept-store-fitness-nyc
8. https://www.styledemocracy.com/lululemon-closes-mens-stores/
9. Ibid.
10. https://www.retailcustomerexperience.com/articles/lululemon-taps-data-intelligence-to-amplify-customer-experience-relationship/
11. https://www.intelligentautomation.network/transformation/articles/lululemon-bet-big-on-digital-technology-and-won-heres-how
12. Ibid.
13. Ibid.
14. https://risnews.com/lululemon-pivots-focus-digital-faced-store-closures-due-coronavirus
15. https://www.cnbc.com/2020/12/15/lululemon-ceo-expects-digital-growth-momentum-to-continue-post-pandemic.html
16. https://timesofindia.indiatimes.com/city/bengaluru/canadas-lululemon-opens-tech-centre-in-bengaluru/articleshow/82298525.cms
17. Ibid.

CHAPTER 8: HUMANIZING
THE EXPERIENCE

1. Kozmo.com Splash page. Kozmo.com. Archived from the original on April 8, 2000. Retrieved July 10, 2010.
2. https://www.failory.com/amazon/kozmo-com
3. Ibid.
4. https://screenrant.com/why-when-myspace-failed/
5. https://www.businessinsider.com/tesla-model-3-y-s-x-delivery-wait-times-months-2021-10
6. https://www.cnbc.com/2021/02/18/tesla-ranks-30th-in-unofficial-debut-on-jd-power-dependability-study.html
7. https://www.cnbc.com/2020/07/22/tesla-porsche-and-dodge-create-the-most-joy-for-owners-says-jd-power.html
8. https://robinhood.com/us/en/support/articles/our-story/
9. https://www.forbes.com/sites/halahtouryalai/2014/02/26/forget-10-trades-meet-robinhood-new-brokerage-targets-millennials-with-little-cash/?sh=14a8faab7f48
10. Ibid.
11. https://www.huffpost.com/entry/startup-insider-the-story_b_7976446
12. Ibid.
13. https://tearsheet.co/future-of-investing/why-robinhood-is-launching-a-social-network/
14. https://www.dynamicyield.com/files/ebooks/DY-Book-Amazon.pdf; B. Smith and G. Linden, "Two Decades of Recommender Systems at Amazon.com," *IEEE Internet Computing* 21, no. 3 (2017): 12–18.
15. https://tearsheet.co/future-of-investing/why-robinhood-is-launching-a-social-network/
16. Ibid.
17. https://www.marketwatch.com/story/robinhood-tempts-savers-with-3-interest-on-checking-accounts-but-should-consumers-hand-over-their-cash-2018-12-13

CHAPTER 9: CONNECTING YOUR
CUSTOMER WITH YOUR CAUSE

1. https://online.hbs.edu/blog/post/corporate-social-responsibility-statistics
2. https://jcsr.springeropen.com/articles/10.1186/s40991-018-0039-y

3. https://www.thebodyshop.com/en-gb/about-us/a/a00001
4. https://phdessay.com/the-body-shop-corporate-social-responsibility/
5. https://bjsocialresponsibility.weebly.com/
6. https://www.forbes.com/sites/effibenmelech/2021/08/01/ben--jerrys-social-responsibility-esg-without-the-g/?sh=351d8f253084
7. https://www.feedough.com/one-for-one-forerunner-toms-shoes-business-model/
8. https://www.toms.com/us/impact.html
9. https://www.aflac.com/docs/about-aflac/csr-survey-assets/2019-aflac-csr-infographic-and-survey.pdf
10. https://onlinemasters.ohio.edu/blog/why-corporate-social-responsibility-matters-in-todays-society/
11. https://www.edelman.com/sites/g/files/aatuss191/files/2018-10/2018_Edelman_Earned_Brand_Global_Report.pdf
12. https://www.forbes.com/sites/forbesagencycouncil/2019/07/01/taking-a-stand-how-brands-are-tackling-social-issues/?sh=726189912e59
13. Ibid.
14. https://www.thomasnet.com/articles/other/amazon-csr-sustainability/
15. https://www.adl.org/resources/tools-and-strategies/nikes-ad-and-believing-in-something
16. https://info.lululemon.com/sustainability/our-footprint
17. https://www.fatbuddhastore.com/patagonia-timeline-i278
18. https://www.patagonia.com/company-history/
19. https://www.fatbuddhastore.com/patagonia-timeline-i278
20. https://www.patagonia.com/stories/
21. https://www.patagonia.com/stories/life-lived-wild/story-102412.html
22. https://www.patagonia.com/stories/was-it-worth-it/story-114556.html
23. https://www.patagonia.com/stories/episode-2-run-to-be-visible/video-103813.html

CHAPTER 10: LOOKING TO THE FUTURE

1. https://www.brainyquote.com/citation/quotes/p_j_orourke_617457
2. https://www.dailymail.co.uk/sciencetech/article-2221363/Google-reveals-Star-Trek-inspired-vision-future-computing.html

3. https://screenrant.com/google-glass-smart-glasses-what-happened-explained/
4. https://en.wikipedia.org/wiki/Apple_Newton#cite_note-Evans-12
5. https://www.wired.com/2013/08/remembering-the-apple-newtons-prophetic-failure-and-lasting-ideals/
6. https://backlinko.com/facebook-users
7. https://www.zdnet.com/article/ai-powered-virtual-assistants-and-future-of-work/
8. Ibid.
9. https://ios.gadgethacks.com/how-to/fast-can-you-really-type-your-iphone-take-these-tests-find-out-0384396/
10. https://www.write-out-loud.com/speech-rate.html
11. Ibid.
12. https://www.wired.com/story/what-is-the-metaverse/
13. https://medium.com/headlineasia/ariana-grande-x-fortnite-rift-tour-the-apogee-of-pop-culture-or-just-the-beginning-5052584f8d63#
14. https://english.alarabiya.net/business/technology/2021/11/30/Around-16-000-people-buy-virtual-plots-of-land-in-Sandbox-metaverse-Co-founder#
15. https://www.yahoo.com/video/three-plots-digital-land-next-163550699.html
16. https://twitter.com/TheSandboxGame/status/1455405812881534980?s=20&t=wIvHS_VzJN8wHPuCicvzGw
17. https://www.tmj4.com/news/local-news/miller-lite-has-entered-the-digital-universe-with-a-metaverse-tavern-virtual-beer
18. https://www.wired.com/story/what-is-the-metaverse/
19. https://www.xrtoday.com/virtual-reality/unpacking-meta-where-did-the-word-metaverse-come-from/
20. https://www.forbes.com/sites/greatspeculations/2021/12/20/the-metaverse-is-a-1-trillion-revenue-opportunity-heres-how-to-invest/?sh=7639b2424df9
21. https://www.altpress.com/meta/history-of-nfts-non-funfible-tokens/
22. https://www.theguardian.com/technology/2021/dec/16/nfts-market-hits-22bn-as-craze-turns-digital-images-into-assets
23. https://www.altpress.com/meta/history-of-nfts-non-funfible-tokens/
24. https://luxurylaunches.com/celebrities/snoop-dogg-virtual-neighbor.php

25. https://www.coca-colacompany.com/news/coca-cola-nft-auction-fetches-more-than-575000
26. Ibid.
27. https://www.theverge.com/22833369/nike-rtfkt-nft-sneaker-shoe-metaverse-company
28. https://www.instagram.com/p/CLzsM1epvFH/
29. https://news.nike.com/news/nike-acquires-rtfkt

About the Author

Steven Soechtig has worked at the intersection of brand and experience for over 30 years. In 1999, while working for Deloitte, Steve was part of a small team that launched the digital agency Roundarch, which addressed the earliest questions around the impact of digital on brand and experience. Steve has also launched two other software startups, Orchestria and Abiquo, each of which offered solutions to improve the customer experience. In 2013, he rejoined Deloitte as a Managing Director and led the creation and expansion of their Digital Experience practice. This led him to join McKinsey as an Expert Partner in the Digital Marketing practice and most recently serving as CEO of Ogilvy Experience, where he led an organization focused on advising clients on the core topics of this book.

Index

INDEX

INDEX

Index

INDEX

INDEX